The Psychic
Casebook

The Psychic Casebook

Real Encounters with the Paranormal

Craig Hamilton-Parker

BLANDFORD

A Blandford Book
First published in the UK 1999 by Blandford

Cassell plc
Wellington House, 125 Strand, London WC2R 0BB
www.cassell.co.uk

A Cassell Imprint

Distributed in the United States by Sterling Publishing Co., Inc.,
387 Park Avenue South, New York, NY 10016-8810

A Cataloguing-in-Publication Data entry for this title is available
from the British Library

ISBN 0-7137-2755-1

Designed by Richard Carr
Printed and bound in Great Britain by MPG Books Ltd, Bodmin, Cornwall

Dedication

This book is dedicated to Sathya Sai Baba,
the omnipresent Indian Avatar who keeps
our egos in check and guides us
to the path of love.

Contents

Introduction

Do not think of the existence of two entities – this world and the next, here and hereafter. Realize that hereafter is here; this world is interwoven with the next.

Sathya Sai Baba

Never before in the history of humanity has so much energy been dedicated to fulfilling material ambitions, collecting possessions and seeking ever more luxurious comfort. In the process many people have lost sight of the spiritual part of their lives and feel that their life is barren of meaning. In this book I have tried to go back to the ancient spiritual source and to show what lies beyond death. I hope it will inspire you to continue your spiritual search for direct insight, inspiration and understanding.

The message that shines through this book is that we need not live in perpetual darkness. Everyone can become attuned to spiritual powers and influences. Everyone has latent powers of ESP (Extra-Sensory Perception), mediumship, clairvoyance, and all can attain divine consciousness.

Many of the case studies you will read here are from people who make no claims to having extraordinary paranormal powers. They are ordinary people who, for some unknown reason, have had a spontaneous clairvoyant insight. You will read of people who have glimpsed the future, communicated by telepathy, travelled out of the body, proved that they have lived before or communicated with the spirit world. In addition you will read of people who have had miraculous experiences, and in particular read about the Indian holy man Sathya Sai Baba whose miracles are being witnessed across the UK, Australia and America.

My sources come from my media work and people I have interviewed during my years as a psychic columnist for various newspapers and magazines in the UK, Australia, America and South Africa. Some stories have been sent to me via my internet web site. In many cases I have changed names and locations so as to protect the identity of the people involved, as there are many sceptics who seek to discredit all things paranormal. There was a time when such people made me angry, and I have appeared on several television debates to defend our corner. Frankly, I don't care anymore. There is plenty of scientific evidence to support my claims. You can read these case studies and make up your own mind. Many of the stories are based upon interviews and letters from my work as a journalist, and have been checked by editors or corroborated by other journalists. The people who have had the courage to tell their stories in these pages are honest individuals.

The stories have been cemented together with case files from my own work as a medium and the work of my psychic wife, Jane. I have included the messages from the famous medium Doris Stokes and also testimonials and case files from sitters who have had a consultation with Jane or myself. I have also included a few fun, psychic experiments that you can try for yourself. For reasons of privacy I have not included information about consultations with celebrities who have seen Jane or myself.

I do not claim to have all the answers. I am not a guru and I can't wave a magic wand and make people's problems disappear. Although I have well-developed mediumistic and psychic abilities, I do not claim to be more spiritual than the next person. Like you, I am also seeking and will continue to seek for the rest of my life. This is what life is about, for as we seek, we grow. On my journey of discovery I have found various treasures, and fellow travellers have shared their experiences about their own search with me. I hope that this book will throw a little light into this dark world, and help guide the way for those who seek spiritual truth.

Chapter One

Media Psychics

(Case file 1)

When Stan and Karen Kopec drove their young daughter Kalle to hospital on Easter weekend in 1992, they had no idea what horrors were to await them over the next few days. As far as they knew Kalle had nothing more than croup. Her mum Karen Kopec says:

> Kalle had just celebrated her birthday and the bright early morning light reminded me of the time, four years ago, when my husband Stan had driven me to the hospital to give birth to her.
>
> Our gentle mood turned to horror when Kalle began to choke at the hospital. She had epiglotitus caused by the hib virus – a similar illness to meningitis that causes severe swelling in the throat – and her attack was so severe that soon she was on a life support machine with all its intimidating tubes, screens and wires.
>
> Kalle lay in intensive care for three days. The doctors broke the news to us: our bright little girl would never recover. The machine was keeping her alive and, in the unlikely event that she would ever regain consciousness, she would be little more than a vegetable. The machine needed to be switched off.

Kalle's father, Stan, takes up the story:

> And there was another painful decision to make. Which one of us would hold her as they switched off the life support? We both so much wanted to hold our little girl. Karen had brought her into this world so it seemed right that Karen should hug her tight as she left.

Karen continues:

> As the bleepers, monitors and lights became still I saw the light fade too from our little princess. I knew that she had gone and what lay limply before me was not our sweet girl anymore. We knew it was now over, but at the same time Stan and I heard a clear voice in our heads: 'I'm not there now, Mummy and Daddy, please go home.'

Stan and Karen were left in a state of shock. Everyone else could express their grief, the house was full of family, friends, and neighbours shedding tears, but the couple were numb with unspoken pain:

> I don't know how we could be so strong. It almost made me feel guilty and, in some ways, frustrated to have to comfort everyone else.
>
> Now I look back, I feel that Kalle knew that she was going to die – even before she became ill. The day she first became poorly I saw a competition in a magazine for children to draw their ideal house so I suggested that Kalle occupy herself by drawing one. Kalle was normally a very talented four-year-old artist, yet she produced a strange picture that, in retrospect, may have been a premonition of her future.

Karen showed me the drawing. Kalle had drawn a large, square, white building with a flat roof that looked like a hospital. Outside of this she drew herself playing in the pink and blue flowers. Through the window on the left was a little girl, who was ill, in an iron bed with bars. This was surrounded by boxes with wires – a picture that represented her future in hospital perhaps? To the right was another large window, but inside there was nothing. It was as if Kalle had been drawing herself in the present and in the future, but the last room, which represented her death, she didn't understand, so in this she drew nothing:

> Another strange thing was that Kalle believed that at night she was being visited by a man called Michael, who she used to talk to in front of me. She loved the music of Michael Jackson and I wondered if this was a fantasy about him. On her headstone we put some of the words from his songs, and now if I listen to the words of 'Heal the World' and 'Will you be there?', her favourite songs that she sang before her illness, the words seem particularly poignant as they are about how beautiful the life is hereafter.

The first communication that Karen and Stan had from Kalle's spirit came in the form of another drawing. A psychic artist, who had never seen a photograph of Kalle, sent the Kopecs a coloured pencil-sketch of how Kalle's spirit looked now. Comparing it to a photograph I could see that there was a striking resemblance – the artist had even drawn the small distinguishing mark on Kalle's cheek. 'The one thing that the psychic artist had got completely wrong, though,' says Karen, 'were the eyes – Kalle had brown eyes not blue ones as the picture showed.'

Prior to her reading with myself, Karen had briefly met another medium. 'He said that he wanted to tell me something from a little girl on the spirit side,' says Karen. '"She says that she's got big blue eyes now!"'

Karen and Stan felt that Kalle had been trying to communicate with them in other ways too. Stan explains:

> We used to see spiralling blue lights in our room, and at other times smelt an overwhelming scent of flowers and a feeling of warmth when we talked about her – a smell that used to follow us then disappear as quickly as it came. After she died, our doctor friend in Australia, who received a phone call saying Kalle had died a few hours earlier, said he knew something had happened because he had seen her figure standing in his bedroom – he didn't even know that Kalle had been ill.

Karen first came for a sitting with myself at a psychic fair. She goes on:

> We only went along because it was raining and we had nothing better to do. Little did I know that it would be a life-changing experience. Craig lay out the Tarot cards but soon pushed them aside saying that he wanted, with my permission, to work with me mediumistically. Although he was tired and the noisy conditions were difficult to work with, there was a lady and a little girl insisting that they talk with me. The lady he described was my aunt, who Craig said was helping with the communication. 'Your little girl is worried about your Mum,' said Craig, 'she's taken her granddaughter's death very badly' – which was quite true. When I spoke to Mum immediately after the reading I realized that her depression over Kalle was far, far more serious than I had realized.
>
> Craig proceeded to give me proof of Kalle's survival of death. He said that she died when she was four but would be six now, and that she died covered in tubes and wires in intensive care on 23 April. She had, he said, a swollen throat, a bad stomach and passed over just after her birthday on 23 March (her birthday was 22 March).
>
> I was stunned as Craig reeled off the facts about Kalle's passing. He said that her name sounds something like Sally, but it was the little things that clinched it. A reading that was supposed to be ten minutes went on for an hour. This was the first time I had got a really positive link with my child and Kalle wasn't going to let Craig go. Tears were running down Craig's cheeks as he made this emotional link.
>
> Craig described Kalle's long brown hair that I had stroked as she lay dying, her favourite red wellies. He talked about her treasured hat with

a flower in the middle, her toy helicopter, her racing car with only three wheels, her allergy to cheese and the old teddy, that used to have a red bow, and which had been put in the coffin with her. There was a little pink teddy with her, too, communicated Kalle – the one that her friend had given her at the hospital.

Kalle sent her love to her dad and my 'dead' aunt interjected to say to stop worrying about the tax bill. Craig said she was talking about Nana, Nana with the bad legs and how she lived next door to the pigs. (Nana, Nana was her pet name for Karen's Grandma who had recently started suffering because of her legs.)

Craig said that Kalle showed him an unfinished dolls' house that her dad had made with its pretty pink furniture and how her brother Stefan now likes to play with her toys, particularly her helicopter. He described a horse in the mud – a horse had once stood on her foot, but the soft mud had prevented any bones being broken.

Kalle went on to say how she loved her brothers Luca and Stefan. And she said she would soon have a new baby sister. I thought there was no way that could be true. I had been told that I should not have any more children, even though I was desperate to have another little girl.

Karen had already had two Caesareans, while an ectopic pregnancy had left her with extensive scarring. A consultant had said another pregnancy would be very risky, as her womb might not be able to hold the baby. However, during another session, I told Karen that she was pregnant with a girl. Although Karen felt this could not possibly be true, she nevertheless found comfort in the sessions. 'They gave us strength because, for the first time, we felt as if Kalle was still with us. Her death nearly ripped the family apart; now we felt we could carry on.' Soon after, to her great joy, Karen found out she *was* pregnant – and a scan confirmed it was a girl. The astounded family eagerly awaited the birth of a very special baby. Kodie was born in November 1995. Karen is delighted:

> This is a dream come true. But although it's wonderful to have another little girl, this doesn't mean that we'll forget about Kalle. When she died, I was so low that I thought I'd never get back up again. But we're slowly getting there.
>
> And I know Kalle is still with us. Just the other night, I asked her for a cuddle and felt her arms around me.

In conclusion Karen says of her brush with mediumistic communication:

Craig, and now Spiritualism, have given Stan and I the courage to carry on. Our mutual suffering has brought us even closer together. Most of all I like to think that Kalle's over there and, although our time together was short, she may think to herself, 'I had two nice parents who adored me.'

Her tragedy has given me an insight into the values of life, and if my story of hope in darkness helps just one mother who feels the way I do, I will be so happy. There is something far better and far greater that's just that little distance away. Kalle has gone home but I know she's always there if I need her.

Karen is one of the bravest mothers I have met. She conquered adversity with dignity and compassion at the loss of her angel Kalle. And I believe that Kalle is indeed an angel. Constant in every account of angels throughout history is that they are both messengers and companions to humans. It is the nature of their office to bring messages of the highest hope, inspiration and comfort to those who suffer on earth. Kalle brought this message to her mother. She has no wings but she is an angel nonetheless.

Our work as mediums is dedicated to proving that there is life after death. Together with my wife Jane, who is also a medium, I believe that we have brought comfort and inspiration to many desperate people, like Karen and Stan, who desperately need to know that there is more to this world than just the commonplace. Jane and I are not New Age gurus, nor do we have all the answers to life's many perplexing questions. Sometimes our clairvoyance and mediumship is accurate and precise, but there are inevitably times when the clear signals from beyond are clouded by our own thoughts.

I am a reluctant medium. Like many people, I had no intention of developing psychic powers; they were thrust upon me. The events of my life sometimes seemed to conspire to push me along this path. It has brought me both joy and woe but, most importantly, it has shown me that beyond the winding pathways of life lies my spiritual homeland.

Developing psychic powers

My mother tells me that I have always been psychic. I used to frighten her when I described the things I saw, such as figures in my bedroom at night, colours around people's heads and dreams that came true. Throughout my life I had an uncanny ability to read people's thoughts and my telepathic abilities used to astonish, and sometimes alarm, my family and friends.

Of course, mediumistic abilities are more than just mind-reading, as I will endeavour to prove. But psychic skills were most certainly evident in both my wife Jane and myself from an early age. In my case they appeared at first haphazardly, and it wasn't until I met the medium and police sergeant Peter Close, who trained me in his circle, that the jigsaw puzzle fell into place. It was as if I had suddenly found what I was searching for all my life and my psychic skills developed at a remarkable rate. Now I knew how to turn the psychic switch on and off and was no longer at the mercy of sometimes unwanted clairvoyant insights. Soon I could give clear and precise evidence of survival and was able to consciously develop my abilities. Teaching psychic self-development has become an integral part of my work today.

Jane's mediumistic development was quite different:

> My grandmother realized that I was a very psychic child. She was very interested in psychic things herself, although not a professional medium, and was able to guide my psychic progress. She would do this at first through guessing games and finally taught me to see pictures in a crystal ball which she helped me to interpret. In this way I was able to understand how to develop ESP from an early age.

By the time Jane and I met we were both mediumistically advanced. It was Jane's dead grandmother who introduced us. I was giving a public demonstration of mediumship and linked with Jane in the audience. I described and named her grandmother Barber in the spirit who insisted that we meet up. We did, and fell in love. We were soon married.

Another person who was partly responsible for our coming together was the late medium Doris Stokes. Thousands thronged to see Doris's public demonstrations of mediumship. She became the world's best-known medium and, in her simple, unassuming way, popularized the knowledge that had previously been limited only to Spiritualists and other similar organizations. She was famous all over the world and could fill the London Palladium or Sydney Opera House to capacity.

When my sister Vivienne lost her husband from cancer soon after she was married, it was Doris who helped take the heavy burden of grief from her shoulders. I went with Viv to the sitting and was astonished at the things Doris also said to me. She 'knew' about my problems as a single parent with a 16-month-old baby to look after, and she described my grandmother in the spirit world and made some predictions about my business, how I would travel and who and when I would marry.

Two predictions came to pass almost instantly. At the time I was running my own advertising agency, and she named a blue chip company that I would be doing work for. A few weeks later, and quite unexpectedly, the company rang me up with a big order that was to put me on a firmer financial footing – Doris had even given me the name of the man who would place the order!

She also said that I would go to America with my long-time friend Stuart Martin. Stuart was then offered a temporary teaching job on an American Youth Camp. As I boarded the plane to LA to meet up with Stuart there I recalled what Doris had said.

The most remarkable prediction that Doris made, although she always said that she couldn't see the future, was concerning my future wife. 'Jane Wallis' was the name she had given. 'You will meet your future wife, Jane Wallis, on 6 March. It took a good few years but it was 6 March that Jane and I met at my mediumistic demonstration. Jane's name was Willis, which was pretty close to Doris's prediction, but her grandmother, who had pulled the strings from the spirit side, had the maiden name of Wallis.

The Stokes family were important in Jane's development as well:

> I got to know John Stokes after Doris Stokes had passed to spirit. He originally came down to my home in Eastleigh to help a friend of mine who needed some spiritual healing – not many people know about John's healing gift. We got on with each other straight away and often used to meet up, together with his adopted son Terry. John was a lovely, kind man and I thought of him as a second father.

Jane's father had died some years ago and when we decided to get married it was John who Jane asked to give her away in church. We wondered if Doris was there too – watching it all from the afterlife. In fact she was, and told us all about it later through another medium.

Mediums can't give themselves readings, as personal thoughts get in the way. If Jane and I want to have a message from spirit we have to visit someone else. We decided to visit a medium when Jane was a few months pregnant with our daughter, Danielle. It wasn't easy to spot she was pregnant.

The medium was David Walton, of whom we had heard, but weren't sure if he was genuine or not. It is very hard to find a gifted medium that gets clear evidence. David, however, proved to be excellent.

We wanted a sitting together even though we knew that most mediums, including ourselves, prefer to work with sitters independently.

There was a cancellation and we were booked in as his last appointment of the day. We were lucky.

'I'm hearing the name Barber,' he said, going straight to Jane's grandmother's name, as I and other mediums had done before. He continued with other good evidence about her and also things about grandad and various other people we remembered who had gone to spirit. It was all excellent evidence.

'I'm feeling that my guide Dominic wants to come through,' David went on. Dominic, we were told later, had been a monk in Brussels over 300 years ago and had first appeared to David when he was 12. Dominic spoke through David Walton with a gentle, kind voice. He spoke slowly and deliberately with an accent quite different to David's.

'Congratulations on the wedding,' were his first words. We had not even had our first anniversary. 'This baby that's coming is very special. It doesn't belong to you. This child belongs to God. It was no coincidence the way you two came together, you two were chosen for each other. The suffering and pain that both of you have had is for a reason.' (Jane had recently nearly died in a major operation.) Dominic then went on:

> You are privileged to have suffered and you have passed the test. On the table in front of you are many spiritual gifts and they are yours for the asking. You two are destined and chosen to do this work for God and to lift the burden of suffering from many. Sometimes you may think that we in the spirit have left you, but we are always there helping you with your work.

He paused a while and then we heard another voice, a lady's voice with a strong Northern accent. 'Fancy seeing you here, love. It's Doris. It was a lovely wedding and John looked so nice beside you. John's not been too well, you know, and I'm a little worried about what's happening to my Terry.' We understood the message as coming from Doris Stokes. Who else would comment on John Stokes or be concerned for their step-child Terry?

When David Walton came out of his trance he was surprised that the spirit guides had put him under. He didn't know us, and certainly would never have realized that we knew Doris, John, and Terry Stokes. We thanked him for a wonderful sitting and drove home to contemplate what we had been told.

Some time after the sitting Jane, who had gone to bed early, came downstairs where I was watching television. She looked pale as she turned off the television and stood in front of the screen to get my attention. 'I've just seen the figure of John Stokes standing in our bedroom,' she said. 'He looked happy, but I'm sure something has happened to him.'

With the hectic schedule we had been keeping we hadn't contacted John for some time. We tried to ring his home, but the number was dead. The next day I was to do a demonstration of mediumship at The Spiritualist Association of Great Britain at Belgrave Square in London. This had been an old haunt of Doris Stokes, so when I got there I asked around to find out if anyone had any news about John. 'Oh, John Stokes,' said one of the resident mediums who shared the meditation room, 'he passed to spirit only a few weeks ago!'

Jane and I believe that, sometimes, particularly when we work with an audience, Doris and John work with us from the other side. Perhaps it is just one of those things that many mediums would like to think, but I am sure that they have joined that band of spirit helpers that guide us and other mediums. I am certain that when it is Jane's and my turn to go over, we will stand right beside them, proving to the people of earth that life really does continue.

Demonstrating Mediumship

When a fledgling medium takes their first hesitant step away from the security of the psychic development circle, it is nerve-racking. Peter Close, my teacher, kindly introduced me to the Spiritualist churches he served in London, where I was able to give my first demonstrations to an audience.

I was very nervous as I stood in front of the congregation at Pembridge Church. It was the first time I had ever been inside a Spiritualist church, let alone taken the service! With much encouragement from Peter, and in front of a sympathetic audience, I soon got into my stride and began giving the details of the spirit communicators. I was amazed at how easily and clearly the information came through. With the right 'conditions', as we mediums say, mediumistic communication is much easier.

Modern Spiritualism is generally considered to date from events which took place in Hydesville, New York State, on 31 March 1848. Two sisters, Margaretta and Catherine Fox, established intelligent communication with a spirit entity which had been responsible for noisy rappings on the walls of their house. A flood of publicity followed and the world's first seances were started in America and, from 1852, in Britain.

The movement began to attract the attention of eminent scientists and intellectuals, including the pioneer of cooperative societies, Robert Owen (1771–1858); the eminent chemist and physicist, Sir William Crookes (1832–191); and the author of the *Sherlock Holmes* stories, Sir Arthur Conan Doyle (1859–1930). Other intellectual giants joined them, and in 1853 the first Spiritualist church was established in England at Keighley, Yorkshire.

Spiritualism proposed that the spirit world was communicating a new revelation, which had important religious implications. In 1937, the then Archbishop of Canterbury, Cosmo Gordon Lang (1864–1945), set up a committee to investigate Spiritualism and produced a favourable report. Although the report was suppressed, it was leaked to *Psychic News* (founded in 1932).

At first it was impossible for mediums to work openly and some mediums, such as Helen Duncan in 1944, were tried and jailed for their beliefs. Spiritualist meetings were raided by the police and the participants prosecuted under the Vagrancy Act of 1824 and the Witchcraft Act of 1735. It wasn't until as late as 1951 that it became legal to practice mediumship.

I discovered the history of Spiritualism only after I had started demonstrating in Spiritualist churches. Initially I had no idea of the extent of Spiritualism, nor of its intellectual pedigree. At a typical Spiritualist service, the medium opens with a prayer and then there is a hymn, followed by a moment of meditation and absent healing (where healing energy is sent to a person in another location). After a short reading, the medium then gives a talk about the philosophical implications of spirit communication. This is followed by another hymn to lift the vibrations and finally the medium gives a demonstration of mediumistic communication for members of the congregation he feels drawn to. When I started I had never seen another platform medium in action, and so my style of working was uniquely my own.

Since my first demonstration I have taken hundreds of Spiritualist services, and today I am confident when giving a talk or demonstrating mediumship to an audience. To give you an idea of what happens at a demonstration, the following is an extract from the newsletter of Wilton Spiritualist Church in Wiltshire:

Visiting medium Craig Hamilton-Parker gave one of the most detailed messages heard in our church at September's meeting. Starting with the name 'Hayward', which was initially unrecognized, he then heard the word 'Britannia'. Keith Williams thought he recognized the details and Craig gave the Christian name of 'Colin'.

Keith explained that he had served in Ulster with a Colin Hayward, who had been singing 'Rule Britannia' just prior to being killed. He had saved his comrades by throwing himself onto an IRA bomb so as to shield the blast. As he did so he sung 'Rule Britannia'. The message continued:

Craig: This took place in Londonderry.
Keith: Correct.
Craig: He had a girlfriend and I feel he was just about to get married.
Keith: He was due to go on leave in nine day's time and would have got married three days after that.
Craig: Do you know if the girl's name was Sally?
Keith: I can't remember. [This was confirmed as correct later.]
Craig: He's talking about Charlie Watts.
Keith: That was his best friend.
Craig: There was also a Tommy in the group he saved. Quite gangling in his appearance.
Keith: That's right.
Craig: He's showing me his cap-badge. It has three feathers on it.
Keith: Yes he was in the Hussars.
Craig: I'm getting 23 September.
Keith: As far as I can remember, he died in late September.

Now that's the sort of evidence Spiritualism really stands on. In my 30 years in the movement, I have rarely heard such detailed 'evidence of identity'.

Well, there's a feather in my cap too!

Unfortunately Spiritualism's glorious past has, in some ways, stopped it progressing. Today most of the intellectuals have deserted it, materialization circles are now extremely rare and even the standards of mental mediumship have deteriorated to superficial psychism. Perhaps Spiritualism is dying away because it has become old-fashioned. The movement is plagued by committees that cannot agree on the simplest agenda for change. The net effect is that Spiritualism can sometimes be boring.

Despite this, however, there are still pockets of excellence within the movement, and in the future these may bring about a reanimation and new momentum. Spiritualism at its best can be tremendously uplifting. Despite its faults it is well worth looking into – maybe you can help change it? I have a great deal to thank Spiritualism for. My teacher Peter Close, himself a Spiritualist, and the Spiritualist church, gave me a platform to practise my skills in front of the public. Without this experience it would have been far more difficult to work as confidently as I do today on television, the radio and through the newspapers.

Jane's early development was quite different. Guided by her grandmother during childhood, the bond continued after she died:

> I've always felt that my grandmother draws close at important times. Sometimes she advises or warns me about events, and there have been occasions when I've heard her voice give such a clear warning that I act upon it. Craig and I have even turned down television shows if my grandmother's spirit has said it's a negative show. She was certainly right when we turned down what looked like a golden opportunity to become well known. The show in question we saw later was hosted by the American conjuror James Randi. He is an arch-sceptic and gave everyone a hard time.

Case file 2

As I was developing a reputation for my public demonstrations, Jane's reputation was spreading because of her private sittings. Before we became professional, we never charged for our public or private work. Jane, I know, has saved many despairing people from the brink of suicide. Sometimes the overwhelming influence of the spirit people and the insistence of her 'dead' grandmother would impel her to rush to people's houses unannounced.

Such an event took place one day in 1972. The telephone directory was lying open on the living room table when Jane saw a vivid blue light flash across it. She picked it up and the blue lights highlighted the name of J. Chivers. Jane continues:

> I knew that something was desperately wrong at this unknown person's house. I felt the spirit of a young boy close to me and heard my grandmother urging that I should go straight away to the address. His father was in desperate need of assistance.

Jane jumped in the taxi and, instead of going to the supermarket as she had planned that afternoon, drove directly to Mr Chivers' address. 'It was a hard house to find, but *en route* I could hear the spirit voice giving me precise directions. Turn left here, right there, straight on at the lights.'

Jim Chivers remembers the day well. 'Jane knocked on our door and said, "Is your name Jim? Have you lost a little boy of fifteen called Tim?"' Jim's young son, Tim, had quite recently been killed in a road accident on his way home from school. He had fallen off his bike as he rode up a hill and was crushed under the wheels of a lorry. The ambulance rushed him to hospital but within four hours he was dead:

> Jane unexpectedly gave me a wealth of evidence that proved that Tim was now safe in the spirit world. My wife Shirley and I could never have made it without the assistance of people like Jane. Over the years, from the evidence of mediums and Spiritualists, I have grown to understand that death is by no means the end. Life does indeed continue and, although I am still depressed sometimes on Tim's birthday, passing and at Christmas, I know that he is safely in God's hands.
>
> I don't think that anybody who has not had a bereavement can explain the loss you feel. Although it's a disgusting and selfish thing to do, I made two attempts at suicide, but realize now that the grief I and my family endured was for a purpose – so that I could understand what others go through and offer help.
>
> The hardest part was driving home from hospital without a son. You know it's happened but can't believe it.
>
> In my despair I turned to my local Christian Church but found no solace there. I realized that the vicars knew nothing about the afterlife, even though they talk about it in their sermons every Sunday.

Jim Chivers sought out other mediums to help him with his grief:

> I saw mediums Phil Thomas and Mary Clifford, and other Spiritualists. Their reassurance and evidence – Tim kept coming through – built my strength further. Now I don't need the evidence. I'm thankful for the guidance that the spirit world has given me through mediums like Jane.

Tim's loss has since opened a wonderful spiritual door for Jim. Once he became stronger he joined a psychic development group and discovered that he too has the gifts of clairvoyance, mediumship and healing. Jim has become a close friend of Jane and me and, since his retirement, has become a superb medium who understands the terrible suffering that many of his own sitters are experiencing. 'My own grief has meaning if it has taught me to lift the burden from another's shoulders,' he concludes.

I know how much Jane's mediumship and the work of the Spiritualists helped Jim come to terms with the loss of his son. Jim is a very sincere man and a follower of the Indian Avatar Sathya Sai Baba (see Chapter Ten). During his time of grief he was very vulnerable and a false psychic could have wrought terrible damage. Fortunately in Jane he met the right person.

(Case file 3)

Unfortunately, there are also many sham psychics around, as the following story, told by Cliff and Sue Pedrick, illustrates. Soon after her aunt, Olive, had died Sue decided to visit a medium to see if Olive could communicate with her:

> I needed to know if I was making the best plans for her mentally hand-icapped son Graham. If only Olive could let me know that she approved of my plans and agreed that what I was doing was in Graham's best interest.

Sue's husband, Cliff, accompanied her to the consultation but wasn't impressed:

> Frankly it was an absolute load of twaddle. The woman said things that could apply to anyone and made a string of predictions – none of which have happened. We came away feeling cheated.

Three months later Sue decided that she'd like to try to contact Olive again, but this time Cliff insisted that they apply some rules:

> We'd read about the Eastleigh-based medium Craig Hamilton-Parker and made an appointment to see him. But this time we weren't going to be taken in. Sue and I agreed that we wouldn't lead the medium or give anything away. We agreed that we would only answer 'yes', 'no' or 'don't know'.

Fortunately Cliff and Sue were pleased by what I told them. Cliff goes on:

> No sooner had I sat down, than Craig told me that he was in touch with my father. He said he saw him with jet black hair like mine but also brilliant blue eyes. 'He eventually died of a chest infection,' said Craig, 'but spoke in whispers because there had been something seri-ously wrong with his throat.'

Just before Cliff's father died he had contracted cancer of the throat and had his voice box removed:

Everything Craig said was true yet I had deliberately given him no clues. I could hardly believe what I was hearing.

Next I turned to Sue and said that I wanted to give her a message from her mother:

Craig told me how she died and gave the date of her death to within a few days. He told me that her pet poodle dog was with her and she was now showing him a picture of Michael Jackson. Mum loved her poodle and, only two days before, my five-year-old son Vincent had impersonated Michael Jackson for the school play.

'She's joking about your middle name,' said Craig. 'Can you understand Yan?' My middle name is Yana, which Dad had chosen because he loved the music of the singer of the same name. Everyone, including Mum, used to pull my leg about it.

Craig went on to say that Mum was telling him to say that I mustn't worry too much about the twins' asthma and that my bad back would improve. Craig then stopped and said that he was going to ask my mother for some information that would give me absolute proof that he was in touch with her. 'She's showing me lots of little silver horseshoes.'

Before Mum died she had worked with me in my catering business. After every wedding she would ask the bride for permission to take a silver horseshoe off the cake for good luck. Mum soon had a huge collection of silver horse shoes.

But the spirit world hadn't finished. There were others who also wanted to communicate. Craig asked me if I knew of a Steve in the spirit world. Of course I did! It was my brother, Steve. Craig described how he had taken his own life. He had taken an overdose and the drugs were medically prescribed but they belonged to someone else.

This was quite correct. Craig went on to describe his character, how he liked motorbikes and how we played his favourite song by Meatloaf at his funeral. The fake medium we'd seen in Fareham was using guesswork but these were hard facts that nobody could deny.

Eventually, when the consultation was almost coming to a close, Aunt Olive made contact. Craig wasn't able to give Olive's name, but he was able to correctly say that she was a somewhat domineering school teacher. We'd played the music from her school assembly at the funeral. 'The music was something about a train,' said Craig. The first line of the song was 'Train whistle blowing'!

He also accurately described her cancer and how her legs had swelled. But the information that really shocked me most was when

Craig said that she was dressed in pink in the coffin. Then Craig turned to Cliff and said, 'And all thanks to you, Cliff, you were the one who dressed her.'

Cliff takes up the story:

> Most people leave jobs like that to the undertakers, but Olive always looked like a million dollars in life and I intended that she see out her last moments in style. I dressed her in her finest jewellery and favourite pink dress and jacket.
>
> Then Craig turned to Sue and said, 'And talking about clothes, you've gone from rags to riches. You're now a regular Imelda Marcos.' Craig was spot-on again. A few months before she died Olive had sold her house and went on a massive shopping spree. Sue inherited her clothes, which included eight unopened boxes of new shoes and about another 40 pairs of used ones.
>
> Craig said that I had had her wedding ring made smaller so that her son Graham could wear it, and that she now had something very important to say. 'She's saying,' said Craig, 'that you've done nothing wrong for Graham. In fact she's very pleased with what you've done and organized.'

This was the vital piece of information that Sue and Cliff had been longing to hear. Although Graham lives in care, Sue and Cliff have made him part of their own family. He comes to stay regularly and particularly loves staying for New Year. Sue concludes:

> We're both convinced now that life goes on after death, but it's equally comforting to know that the people we love who've passed over can see and comment on the work that we continue in their memory.

As Cliff and Sue's story illustrates, you have to be wary of which clairvoyant you choose to see. A bad one or an outright charlatan can put you off for life. I myself have been told some terrible things by the fakes. When I was an adolescent a 'psychic' told me that I would break my back before I was twenty. Another said that I would die of lung cancer, while another said that I would lose a leg. Yet another said that I would have my stomach removed. (Thankfully they left me with the important bits.) In each case they were not able to give me any evidence to prove that what they were saying had substance. They did not tell me anything about my past or present, yet made these grim, outlandish predictions about my future.

Jane had a similar experience with a 'clairvoyant'. 'You're having an affair,' the seer said with utmost confidence. Jane became quite angry with her, as she fervently believes that infidelity is wrong, and told her she was wrong. The clairvoyant's reply was, 'Well that surprises me, nearly everyone that comes to see me does.' Clearly this seer was using guesswork.

Case file 4

Bad psychics will never say that they have got something wrong and will attempt to make things fit with the flimsiest of evidence. We all get it wrong sometimes, or get our lines crossed. Jane and I can immediately spot a bad clairvoyant, but visiting someone like this can be really upsetting for someone who assumes that the person giving the reading has an infallible gift. Susie Fabian had such an experience:

> My life was a mess and everything was going wrong. I was deeply depressed and didn't know where to turn. In desperation I decided to visit a psychic. But what the psychic told me was so terribly upsetting – in fact quite terrifying – that I cried all the way home.
>
> She would listen carefully to what I gave away and feed it back to me later in the consultation. For example, I mentioned that I lived in the countryside. Ten minutes later she told me that there were horses near where I lived and I should drive a Land Rover. She fished for information and then started predicting the most frightening things that were to happen: I'd lose my job, husband, home, money, health – you name it, I'd be losing it. 'I'd like to tell you something positive, my dear, but I can't,' said the seer.

For ages Susie kept what she was told to herself.

> I worried about what I had been told day and night. It wasn't until I shared my feelings with my close friend Liz that I began to see how I'd been conned. I played her the tape and we soon realized when we analysed it that she was telling me things I'd already mentioned earlier.

Angrily Susie's friend destroyed the tape in front of her:

> But despite this bad encounter I still wanted to see a psychic and Liz recommended Craig. He had seen many of her friends.

Craig explained that he wanted firstly to communicate with the spirit world and ask them about my life. He started telling me about my mother, who had died a few years ago. He said how she hadn't changed much and even though money was not important where she was, she still worried about it as she was penniless when she died. He told me when she died, how she died, named names and what she was like as a person. Mum laughed about Dad – how he lived on sandwiches, refused to budge from the house and told me lots of stories of things that happened in my life. These were absolutely accurate and no one in a million years could guess the facts but also they are very personal to me and I would rather keep them to myself. Suffice it is to say – I knew by now that some, but not all, psychics are true.

After the mediumistic work, I offered to use Tarot cards to look into Susie's future. While I am first and foremost a medium, sometimes people need a little extra guidance. I believe that the future is subject to our own free will – we can change it. Many mediums disagree with fortune-telling because of the harrowing stories you hear of deception. In the right hands Tarot cards can be a useful tool – but that is all they are, a tool to help with precognition. I see them as a way to compose a philosophy that the sitter can apply to their circumstances. Ultimately the future is what you make it.

The oracle showed problems ahead for Susie, but they weren't impossible. With the guidance of spirit Susie made a plan of action to make the best of the circumstances. I believe that if you sincerely put love behind your actions, then you will do the right thing and, in time, will reap the benefit. It is the natural law of things. Susie concludes:

I left Craig's house on a high. Inside I felt at peace with myself. I knew that there were problems to deal with in my life. It wasn't going to be a bed of roses, but now I could cope.

Next Week's News Today

A career as a full-time medium is not easy. If you are sincere in your work, then it is not possible to work every day – you need time to recharge or you burn yourself out. Even if your schedule is full, people fail to turn up or you feel that you can't charge them because they are in difficulties. It was important that Jane and I developed another string to our bow. As I had advertising and copywriting skills, and understood public relations, my thoughts turned to writing and television.

Our big break came when Bob Geldof's television production company Planet 24 rang us to audition for a new breakfast programme, *The Big Breakfast*. We were to be their resident psychics. Each week we would appear with Paula Yates and predict the coming week's news headlines.

At the audition, Jane and I gave private sittings to two of the most sceptical producers so that they could ascertain whether we were really psychic or not before we did a screen test. Both of them were shaken by how much we could tell them about their lives, and people they knew in the spirit. Indeed, the young man to whom I gave a reading was so emotionally overwhelmed that he requested time off work to come to terms with what he had experienced.

Next we did a screen test to camera, in which we made our predictions for the coming week. The camera crew laughed when Jane said that one of the Queen's corgis would die, but this prophesy and most of the other predictions we made all came to pass within the week. We got the job.

I am sure Paula Yates was just itching to tear us apart from the moment she first saw us come onto the brightly coloured set to the tones of the music from *The Twilight Zone*. It is her Taurean instinct. But time after time our predictions were spot-on and soon even she accepted that what we were doing could not be dismissed as clever guesswork. We foresaw world events with an accuracy that amazed everyone, including sometimes ourselves. During that year, we predicted the El Al air tragedy in Holland; the birth of 'miracle' Siamese twins who were separated; the marriage of Princess Anne in Scotland; the Queen being hit by an egg; the contamination of haemophiliac blood in France; men walking to the South Pole; Elizabeth Taylor's heart attack; the discovery of Rembrandt drawings; the mock assassination attempt on Ross Perot; the French farmers' lamb protest; Cliff Richard losing his voice; a boy being impaled on railings; the arrest of Mafia boss Toto; English footballer Paul Gascoigne getting a black eye; the suicide of American cult leader David Koresh; British politician Chris Patten's heart attack; the horse-ripper attacks; the collision of oil tankers off the Indonesian coast; an unscheduled meeting between the Queen and Boris Yeltsin.

Chris Evans, Paula Yates, Gabby Rosslyn, the crew and even the owner Waheed Ali all became very interested in what we were doing, and occasionally asked for predictions about their own lives. Chris told us that he was quite open to psychic things ever since his mother had become very interested in spiritual healing.

Soon our faces were familiar to British viewers, and there followed a flood of television offers from companies interested in our psychic and mediumistic work. Working for regional, network and cable companies, we soon found ourselves being driven or flown all over the country to take part in various features with a paranormal theme. Some of our predictions on Channel Four were screened on Fox Television in America.

We did the chat shows – comfy pink settees at the crack of dawn. And inevitably we would be asked to demonstrate our psychic skills to titillate the viewers. For *This Morning* with Richard Madeley we demonstrated flower reading and psychometry successfully, and then gave psychic readings to people who rang the show. We were told not to do mediumship as 'it may be a little too serious for a light entertainment show'. Given the pressure there was to 'perform', our accuracy on the phone was very good.

Richard Madeley felt quite armoured against psychic phenomena. He admitted that, like most people with a journalistic or media training, he was taught to be sceptical. However, he thought that we had 'tremendous guts' standing up in front of a camera and doing what we do. On the same show, journalist and former editor of the *Daily Express*, Eve Pollard, was promoting a new book. She was sociable, humorous and apparently open-minded about the existence of ESP.

Fortunately before we went on *This Morning* we had already had practice at phone-ins. For nearly a year we had given telephone readings over the air for our local commercial radio station, South Coast Radio. In this case it was a late-night show, and nobody minded if we talked about the spirit world or demonstrated mediumship. If only mainstream television were so open-minded!

For *The Cheryl Buggy Show* we were able to give some really uplifting evidence of survival. It was the sort material that could bring a lump to your throat. Sometimes we were able to give the full names of the spirit communicator, how they died and an accurate description of their personality. In addition we were able to give exact evidence of stories from their lives. For example, one caller challenged us to say which musical instrument her father had played before he died. 'The bagpipes!' chirped up Jane. We were also able to tell another caller that he had a leg missing, and another that she was looking at a picture of her mother as she spoke. All we had as a 'link' was an unfamiliar voice at the end of the phone line, and the guidance of spirit. Every time we appeared on this show the switchboard was jammed with calls.

We demonstrated psychometry and did a live phone-in on Meridian Television's *Late Night Live*. For this somewhat hectic show we read the vibrations from various objects including a glass eye! On set we also met our old friend Graham Rogers, whom we had got to know when we gave guest appearances on his all-night link programme *Night-time*.

We did a series of shows for *UK Living* with Jane Irving, where we demonstrated aura reading, took telephone calls and interpreted dreams. For *The Vanessa Show* we gave readings to people in the audience and interpreted what they were feeling by the colours of their aura. Afterwards there was a heated debate. One man became quite irate insisting that people like us are frauds. Everyone let off steam – it was an exciting show.

We appeared on the *Richard and Judy* chat show and on the *Daily Mirror's* cable programme *L!VE TV*. I taught astral projection and Jane demonstrated how to use the crystal ball. Normally in television what you say is edited down to just a few minutes, but on cable you pretty well have as much time as you like. I even went on BBC2's *Newsnight* to make predictions about the General Election.

One show that was a complete disaster was Sky's *One to Three*. I had written a feature called 'The Twilight Bone' for *The Sunday Mirror*, in which I related various stories that put forward the idea that pets have a sixth sense. I was approached by the programme producers, who suggested that we set up an experiment in which Jane and I would use telepathy to will a hungry dog to eat from the bowl of our choice. Unfortunately, the dog in question's owner had fed him just before he came on and, to our horror, continued feeding him titbits right up to the moment we released him for the experiment. The dog took no interest in the food whatsoever.

It soon became clear to us that British television is divided into two distinctive camps: 'entertainment' and 'documentary'. Production companies rarely make serious programmes about the type of work we do, and even the investigative programmes still have to be 'entertaining'. It is terribly frustrating when you consider the spiritual implications of what we are trying to say.

Just as the Spiritualists have discovered to their cost, the media aren't interested in the philosophical gauntlet which the proof of life after death throws into the arena. It is almost impossible to put forward a case for mediumship. For a long time the BBC refused to screen anything remotely connected with clairvoyance or mediumship. Even today, a contrary viewpoint from the sceptics always has to be put forward at the same time. I wonder how the public would react if it was mandatory that every time a clergyman expressed an opinion on air, an atheist, psychologist or magician then had to give an alternative viewpoint. I can see it in the listings: '*Songs of Praise*. Tonight's programme includes a talk by the archbishop and a demonstration of walking on water by James Randi.'

As we have never had a theatrical agent, it is perhaps inevitable that we have never been paid particularly well for our television work. Moreover, although the entertainment programmes were fun and useful, what we really wanted was to reach out to people and let them know about the serious and compassionate side of our work.

An opportunity to do this came firstly through the newspapers, when I signed a contract with *The Scottish Daily Record* for Jane and I to write a column, based on an idea which I had proposed to them, called 'The Psychic Postbag'. It would answer readers' questions about psychic subjects and quote their experiences. The resulting weekly Saturday page was flooded with letters telling amazing stories. The Scots, perhaps because of their Celtic roots and the tradition of Highland seership, were very open to what we had to say and 'The Psychic Postbag' became a lively, informative and sometimes touching column. Throughout Scotland it caused quite a stir.

When a Grampian Television producer in Aberdeen, who had read the column, suggested that I host a serious debate on a programme called *We the Jury*, I was delighted at last to be able to put forward some serious ideas. The theme we chose was, 'Is there life after death?'. I would put forward my argument, and then a well-known journalist would put a contrary viewpoint.

For my witnesses I called doctors (who spoke about out-of-body experiences), Spiritualists, Swedenborg followers, members of the Society of Psychical Research and representatives of different faiths. I had planned the debate well, and the sceptics, psychologists and magicians in the opposing camp were soon demolished. The telephone poll that was to decide the winner of the debate went overwhelmingly in my favour. In fact, the presenter said that it was the biggest majority the programme had ever seen. Perhaps programme-makers should note that the public are really very interested in the philosophical implications of clairvoyance and mediumship.

Soon after this programme we were both whisked off to Scotland to be the main guests on Scottish Television's popular programme, *Scottish Women*. I demonstrated mediumship to the audience and gave some convincing proof. Jane gave private consultations to members of the audience selected by the producers. Again without telling us, the same person was also given a 'Tarot' reading by a psychologist posing as a clairvoyant.

Afterwards the people who had been given the readings were asked for their opinions. They had no idea that the other reader was a psychologist. Everyone agreed that Jane's reading was accurate, but that the psychologist had said things that were so general they could apply to anyone. When my mediumistic demonstration was picked apart, it was found that everything I had said was perfectly correct. Once again Jane and I had confounded the sceptics.

I can understand why so many psychics and mediums find that their powers aren't there when they try and demonstrate on television. Producers are sneaky. They tell you that they are making a sympathetic programme and then confront you with psychologists, sceptics and debunkers. You never know what to expect and consequently most psychics are understandably unnerved when this type of thing happens to them on a show. Fortunately, Jane and I have now done so much television that it now takes quite a lot for us fail. Most of the time we know what to expect.

Another debate that I enjoyed was filmed in Birmingham for *Central Tonight*. It was a lively debate, which I co-hosted with another medium Stephen O'Brian. We argued our case against the unlikely bedfellows of Dr Susan Blackmore, a psychologist from Bristol University, and a vicar. Susan Blackmore put forward the usual psychological arguments about hallucinations caused by the temporal lobes, and the vicar told everyone what an evil lot we are.

Then they packed me off to a location where a local psychic had said that a murder had taken place. I was supposed to find the body. I felt nothing and as far as I was concerned the local medium had got it wrong. I met the mother of the murdered girl and I remember telling her that a place with the name of Cromwell was important. At the time the name meant nothing, but a few years later dead bodies were discovered at Cromwell Road in nearby Gloucester. They were the victims of the serial killers Fred and Rosemary West. However, I have had no direct confirmation that the young girl was one of their serial victims.

This was not the first occasion that we have been asked to use our psychic powers in conjunction with a murder. Winnie Johnson lost her son, Keith, to the serial killers Ian Brady and Myra Hindley. She contacted us through *The Big Breakfast* to see if we could help her find her son's body that had been hidden on the moors since the 1960s. Winnie spoke to Jane, who was able to tell her a few things about her son over the phone that had never been revealed, such as the fact that he was on his way to the opticians on the day he was abducted.

Jane was able to relay a few of her feelings about the whereabouts of the body, but Saddleworth Moors is a huge, bleak place and Keith's body remains unfound. It is heartbreaking that poor Winnie Johnson has scoured the moors every weekend since she lost her son in 1964. She said to Jane, 'If I could just hug my little boy's bones I would be at peace.'

One of our best shows together was *Something Strange* for HTV in Bristol. We were billed as mediums and were given the opportunity to demonstrate what we are best at – mediumship. We both gave very accurate proof of who we were communicating with, and gave the correct names of the spirit person being described. I told one lady in the audience, 'Your mother's in the spirit. Her name is Alice and she tells me that you have just bought a small yacht and are soon going to open a delicatessen.' This was correct. Jane told of 'a fireman who had just hurt his back in a skiing accident'. This was also correct.

Again there was the obligatory sceptic. This time they employed a magician who demonstrated sleight of hand to 'prove' that mediums, and particularly materialization mediums, can employ trickery. Frankly, to put forward an argument based upon a few camera tricks was ridiculous and the audience knew it. I believe that all the clairvoyants and mediums who took part collectively gave some pretty convincing proof that it really is possible to prove that there is life after death.

Working under the hot lights of the studio and being told where to walk and stand, and exactly when and how long to speak, is of course, not the perfect way to demonstrate mediumship. Television producers have no idea how ambient and subtle the spirit voices can be. They wrongly assume that we can switch our powers off and on to order. So when the makers of a programme called *The Magic and Mystery Show* asked if they could film my circle conducting a seance I was delighted. This time I could demonstrate mediumship on my own territory and surrounded by the supporting vibrations of my circle members. We would have what Spiritualists call the 'right conditions'.

We used the same fourteenth-century hall in which I hold my weekly meetings, lowered the lights and tried to film discreetly as I conducted the seance. Next to me was sitting the sceptical psychologist Dr Richard Wiseman, and opposite me was the programme's presenter Nick Knowles, to whom I was to give proof of life after death

I opened my circle in the usual way, talking the group through opening the psychic centres, and we entered the silence of meditation. The energy in the room began to build. I resisted trance but held myself on the brink as I gave a spirit message to Nick Knowles. As I linked in I could tell that Nick didn't know many people who had died, but I felt someone draw close to me who was really close to him. 'There's a young man you know in the spirit,' I said. 'He liked motorcycles.'

'Yes,' replied Nick, as Dr Wiseman sat next to me scribbling notes.

'He tells me that he died in Australia and that his name is ***** *****. 'Nick nearly fell off his seat as I gave him the first name and surname of his friend whose grave he specially visited in Australia. 'He says that he was recently engaged to a girl called **** before he died. Her birthday is ****. He sends his love and talks about children by the names of **** and ****. You will be going to America soon.'

Everything I had said was absolutely correct, except Nick had not yet made plans to visit America. I wasn't going to give them a chance to edit out the important bits so I shut up and told them that the power had now left me. I had learned by now that television producers will always edit what you say down to about three to four minutes at the most. They had to use all of what I had said or cut it all.

All Richard Wiseman could argue was that if mediums get something wrong they say, 'Oh, well, that must be something for the future.' But I had only spoken of America as in the future and there was no way I could have cheated. I also had no idea who Nick Knowles was until he arrived, and apparently the company had only decided to use him at the last minute. Furthermore, the spirit communicator wasn't a member of the Knowles family, so he would not have appeared in Nick's family tree. It was impossible for Richard Wiseman to explain away how I knew these names and facts.

In the end the programme nearly didn't get transmitted at all. I was told that what I had said was so accurate that it could upset surviving relatives of Nick's dead friend. In order to show my section, the programme was moved to a late-night slot and they used a bleep to blank out the names and facts when I spoke to Nick. An overdubbed voice explained that I'd given correct Christian names, surnames, locations and dates during my reading. But it wasn't quite the same.

I met Nick again some time later when I was invited to do a telepathy experiment for a show called *Put it to the Test* with Carol Vorderman. Nick admitted that he had been extremely sceptical at first, but that what I had said on *The Magic and Mystery Show* had astonished him. I blew his socks off again when I did the telepathy test and described in accurate detail what was happening in a clip of film that was being shown only to the studio audience. There was absolutely no cheating and a member of staff sat with me in the green room to ensure that there was no way I could inadvertently overhear conversations about what they intended to do. The film showed a scrap-car race with some cars in flames which I described as, 'I feel confined, like I am in a roller coaster, but there are cars and flames flying. Whatever it is, I am moving very fast. It is dangerous but exciting.' I did a similar and successful telepathy experiment with an audience on another regional show called the *Workhouse* for Anglia Television.

Our biggest television triumph came when London Weekend Television approached us about making a programme. The producer Peter Davy told us that they had seen my first book *The Psychic Workbook* (Vermilion, 1995) and felt that some of the ideas in it would make an interesting television programme.

The show would pit us and other psychics, astrologers and clairvoyants against pundits like Simon Hoggart, Angus 'Statto' Loughran and the *Daily Mail* columnist Nigel Dempster, to see who could make the more accurate predictions. Our answers to a range of questions about the future would be locked in a secret vault for six months and unveiled on the show. Hosted by Philip Schofield, this programme would be shown at peak-time on a Saturday evening, and would reach a mass audience.

In the January they filmed us making our predictions at the exclusive Hempel Hotel in London. Six months later the vaults were unlocked and the predictions we had filmed were compared with what had happened in reality. By the time it came to the show, we had forgotten what things we had said to camera six months ago. I know my heart was pounding, and so was Jane's, as they replayed the film. We had got a few very minor things wrong, but overall we scored a resounding success with many direct hits. The astrologers and other psychics who took part also did very well. Nigel Dempster and his team of pundits were right with many of the general trends, but way out when it came to the specifics.

Jane's successful predictions made for 1997 on this programme included: Michael Jackson will have a son; Mandy Allwood will get pregnant; Liam Gallagher will marry Patsy Kensit; David Janson will win a Bafta Award; Victoria from the Spice girls will get engaged. Mine included: Pamela Anderson will be treated by psychologists for depression; the England football team will win 2–0 to Georgia; a car will be hit by a small meteorite.

We also filmed many other predictions which came true, but these were edited out because of time. They included the floods in

Bangladesh and the breach of security in the grounds of Buckingham Palace.

Unfortunately, because television is concerned with entertainment, the real message that we are trying to convey often gets lost amid the glitter and glamour. Our mentor Doris Stokes knew this and made sure people understood the difference between psychic and mediumistic powers. She made it plain that she couldn't tell the future. She could of course, but by saying this it made television producers and the public focus on the real message of her work, which is that the human personality survives death. Predictions such as the football results could be left to the astrologers and card readers. I too have learned how television can turn profound philosophy into cheap, titillating entertainment.

I was, however, pleased when Channel 5 rang me up to ask if I would appear on their *Expresso* programme and demonstrate my mediumistic powers. The person I was to give a reading to on air was Ellen Jameson who is best known for co-hosting a Radio 2 show with husband Derek. To her astonishment, and mine too, I suddenly felt Doris Stokes with me. The *Daily Mirror* published a feature article about what happened. Ellen told them:

> Craig knew nothing about my link with Doris, but she came through to me on the show. He said that Doris was telling him that the first words she ever said to me were, 'I'm not a Tarot reader you know'. I remember the first thing Doris ever said to me was, 'Stop doing the Tarot cards,' and I nearly jumped out of my skin. I was dabbling with them because I'd recently lost my Mum and I was in turmoil. I suppose I was desperate and I'd always been interested in finding out more about the psychic world. We had a sitting together and Doris helped me actually 'see' my Mum and hold a conversation with her. We talked about a dancing clown musical box I've had since I was a child that plays the tune 'Send in the Clowns'. Mum was trying to cheer me up, and, over the years the music box has started up several times of its own accord whenever I've been feeling tearful.
>
> Craig also said that Doris was saying, 'You're a chocaholic, but you're doing well'. I was astounded because nobody knew I had battled to give up chocolate two years earlier. Craig also went on to say that I was in the process of painting my living room in a shocking shade of fuchsia, which was also correct.
>
> He then said that Doris had 'opened the door' and let my father through, and gave an amazingly accurate description of him. He described Dad as a small man who'd had trouble with his legs before

he died, and said that he was quite foggy when he passed over. That was spot-on and I was very moved.

I don't know how I would cope with the loss of a loved one without my trust in mediums. It would seem very strange not to be able to contact the other side.

It was wonderful to communicate with Doris when I was with Ellen. It was clear the two of them are very close and Doris wanted to comfort Ellen by passing on news of her father. It is wonderful when the spirits can help us in this life, and I think you are a very lucky person if you have a friend in the spirit world.

Chapter Two
Telepathic Psychic Powers

It can happen between lovers, friends, family or even with a pet. Telepathy is a mind-to-mind communication that has been with us since before language was invented. The Aborigines of Australia still use this ancient skill to communicate with each other over great distances. Many hunting tribes in Africa and South America 'call' the animals to the hunt using mental powers. For example, fishermen hunting tuna still entice the fish into their nets by mental command, and to this day the chief shaman of the Gilbert Islands in the West Pacific has retained the hereditary title of 'porpoise caller'. His duty, which he enacts at auspicious festival times, is to call the dolphins by telepathy.

Most people are telepathic to some degree, but they either pay little attention to their powers, or don't realize they are displaying anything remarkable. If you have ever finished someone's sentence for them, or have said the same thing as someone else simultaneously, you may have displayed these mind-reading skills.

Have you ever known who's calling even before you answer the phone? This experience is very common and you may notice that it will happen mostly when friends or family ring, but not if the call is from a stranger. This is because the powers of telepathy work best between people who like each other or, better still, love each other. Laboratory tests have indicated that this is the case, and if it happens to you it is a good sign that a friendship or relationship is on the right track.

Telepathic bonding may have a survival function associated with falling in love and choosing the right mate. Once a strong telepathic bonding has been established, the information communicated between the individuals increases beyond the level of just feeling, and will include shared imagery and thoughts. You probably already have these telepathic powers, and with a little help and development, they could assist you in your life.

Telepathy is a Greek word. *Tele* means 'from a distance' and *pathy* stems from the verb 'to feel'. It is a perfectly natural skill that has been neglected and now lies dormant within the mind. Just as telepathy traditionally happens between members of a tribe, so we see its influence in modern Western society. This ancient skill is active at work, in the home, between lovers, and in all areas of life. Most people are unaware that it is happening at all. However, if you scrutinize some of the events in your life, you may find that telepathy is happening more often than you thought. The following sections will explore the secret workings of telepathy, which influences you in mysterious ways that you may never have thought possible.

Telepathy at work

In pre-language societies teamwork was very important, particularly at dangerous times such as the hunt or during tribal wars. A group of hunters would need to be aware of each other's position in relation to the quarry, and they would need to be able to anticipate each other's moves. Sometimes the chase would take place over many miles, and it would have been very difficult to liaise with each other. In these situations humans with a telepathic ability would have had the evolutionary edge.

The modern workplace can be likened to the hunt – although nowadays it is profit we seek rather than prey. Team-building, which today is recognized as an essential and modern management strategy, includes military and hunting terminology such as 'targets', 'strategy', and 'objectives'. In the stock market, terms such as 'bull', 'bear' and 'stag' markets are used. Given that telepathy was usually active for our ancestors during the hunt, it is not surprising that it can often play a role in the modern workplace.

Psychic researcher Betty Humphrey from Duke University, North Carolina, discovered that extrovert personalities displayed better telepathic powers than introverts. Consequently the extrovert salesman or manager is more likely to be receptive to, and able to project, telepathy. For example, telepathic people will trust their gut feeling when employing a new member of staff or establishing a business partnership. So if you are looking for work, project good thoughts towards your potential employer. Their unconscious may respond to your telepathic signals and instinctively they will be more likely to trust you.

The evil Russian monk Rasputin (c.1871–1916) is said to have had hypnotic powers that he could project telepathically. Later, during the Cold War after World War II, both the Russians and the CIA employed telepaths to 'remote influence' enemy world leaders. Such telepathic powers of persuasion may also be used unconsciously by a commanding businessman. Studies have also suggested that telepathic people are often more successful in business and make better leaders.

It has also been established that gamblers and risk-takers display higher than average telepathic abilities and score above chance in telepathy card-guessing tests. The archetypal risk-taking entrepreneur is likely to be unconsciously using these skills for his day-to-day decisions. For example, a hunch about the stock market may be triggered by a perception of collective thoughts being transmitted by people at financial markets around the world.

However, it is imaginative, creative people, and particularly artists, who score best in telepathy tests. Some researchers believe that this is because telepathic people predominately use the right-hand side of the brain – the side responsible for intuition. Some of the most influential businessmen and politicians started their careers from creative media and advertising backgrounds.

TIPS FOR BETTER TELEPATHY AT WORK:
1. Express the extrovert side of your personality.
2. Trust your gut feelings about people and business hunches.
3. Realize that your own thoughts can directly influence others.
4. Try to be creative with your thinking.

Telepathy and relationships

Your most startling experiences of telepathy may have taken place when you were in love. Lovers naturally share thoughts and are sometimes so in tune with each other that they finish each other's sentences, or say the same thing at the same time. When they are apart they 'know' when their partner is thinking of them, if they are feeling sad or worried. Lovers may buy each other the same presents, or independently make the same plans. Science has already shown that people in love copy each other's body language, but there is now evidence to suggest that their brain patterns mimic each other as well. Lovers are literally on the same wavelength.

Laboratory experiments using card-guessing techniques were first conceived by the American scientist Joseph Banks Rhine in the 1930s. They have shown that telepathic abilities appear to increase if the 'receiver' and 'sender' like each other. It has also been found that the attitude of the scientist conducting the experiment may also affect the results. In short, people who trust each other and get on well can telepathically communicate with each other more easily than those who do not like one another. This is amplified even more when we are in love.

There is evidence to suggest that lovers who say that they know what their partner is feeling at a given time may be experiencing telepathy over a distance. It has been found that telepathy appears to take place over any distance. One of the most famous experiments in distant telepathic communication was conducted in 1971 by Edgar Mitchell aboard the Apollo 14 moon mission. In a secret experiment Mitchell beamed images to a 'receiver' on earth. The results did show evidence of ESP, although too few tests were completed for the experiment to be conclusive. NASA had also made last-minute changes to the astronaut's sleeping routines, which disrupted the timing of some of the experiments.

The telepathic bonding between lovers has been recognized throughout history. The Tantric sexual yoga texts from India and Tibet say that telepathic powers are triggered by sexual energy. There is also mention of telepathic thought-sharing in the Japanese and Chinese 'pillow books', such as the *Ishinpoo*, which teach lovers how to use their sexual energies to achieve an ecstatic union of body and soul. In India the infamous *Karma Sutra*, *Koka Shastra* and the *Ananga Raga* all link sexuality with paranormal powers of the mind.

Lovers are also more likely to believe in the telepathy that they spontaneously share and it will be seen as a sign that the relationship is going well. Some scientists have said that people who believe in telepathic powers display higher abilities than those who don't. In short, telepathy works best between people who believe in telepathic powers and who care for each other.

TIPS FOR BETTER TELEPATHY BETWEEN PARTNERS:
1. Recognize that the more you care for each other the more thoughts you will share.
2. Believe that your powers are real.
3. Try ringing your partner at odd times to ask how they are feeling.
4. Be aware of how often you say the same things at the same time.

Telepathy at home

The family environment is the most likely place you will have your first telepathic experience, for it is here that the powers of love are manifest between partners, children and even pets. In particular, telepathic bonding may be an important evolutionary function for the protection of the young.

Many young mothers say that they feel a telepathic link with their new-born babies and tests by psychologists have confirmed this. Experiments have shown that if a sleeping baby is put into a sound-proof room, its mother's heartbeat will increase the moment it wakes up, even though there is no way the mother could have actually heard its cries. Furthermore it has been suggested by psychiatrist Jan Ehren-wald that telepathy is a pre-language survival aptitude which occurs between mother and infant during the dependent period before the child acquires language. Once verbal communication is mastered, tele-pathic communication is no longer fundamental to survival, and the ability is either suppressed or lost.

Fathers can also have a telepathic bonding with their children. It is a popular misconception that women are more psychic than men, and laboratory tests have shown that they have equal telepathic powers. However, women are much more likely to talk about their experiences than men, and 85 per cent of people who report paranormal events are indeed female.

Within the home telepathic thoughts are being shared all the time. Perhaps you have noticed how moods, both good and bad, are almost infectious at home. One of the children starts to play up and soon everybody is upset. Admittedly this is mainly due to normal human reactions, but have you noticed how more intuitively sensitive you are to your family's moods and feelings? Laboratory tests under-taken from 1992 at Edinburgh University by Charles Honerton and Darryl Bern have demonstrated that moods, feelings, and emotions are easier to communicate by telepathy than by words, pictures or numbers.

In a happy home even the pets and plants may respond to the thoughts vibrating around the house. Rupert Sheldrake is currently accumulating a wealth of evidence to suggest that pets respond to their owner's thoughts. For example, they may know when their owner is coming home or even obey mental commands you send them. Perhaps the strangest effect of telepathy will be seen in your household plants. In the 1960s Clive Baxter showed that plants wired to a lie detector will respond to mental thoughts projected at it. Positive thoughts make plants grow, while negative thoughts make them wilt. Given that telepathy is at work within the home, you may be able to tell if it's a happy place by the state of the plants.

Tips for better telepathy at home
1. Try to guess what mood your partner is in before they come home.
2. See if your children will respond to your mental commands. For example, think about sweets and see if they ask you for some.
3. Remember that telepathy works best on an emotional level – notice how your moods unconsciously affect other people.
4. Observe the family pet if you have one. For example, is the dog waiting for you at the window when you return home?

Telepathy for protection

Have you ever been aware that someone is staring at you? Again, this may be another situation where telepathy is at work. Some interesting results from laboratory tests over recent years indicate that many people know when someone is staring at them. A typical 'remote staring' experiment involves situating the participant in a shielded chamber while someone else stares at them via a closed-circuit video. The pulse, and physiological and psychological responses are then monitored to see whether the person is aware of when they are being watched. Establishments such as the Koestler Chair of Parapsychology at Edinburgh University, the University of Utrecht and Duke University and the University of Nevada in the USA are establishing a body of evidence to prove scientifically the reality of telepathy.

This power would have been very useful when man lived in the wild, telling him if a predator was stalking him. Today humans experience these ancient instincts in the unconscious realization that someone is staring. You may draw on these same powers when, for no apparent reason, you feel uncomfortable or threatened by certain people. It is likely that you are sensing that they may mean you harm. This gut feeling is based upon the telepathic impressions you are unconsciously receiving.

It has been found that telepathically gifted people are usually cheerful and sensitive. You may find that your moods are easily affected by the people around you. If you are like this, then it is important to trust these impressions you are receiving.

Quiz

Test your mind-reading powers

Simply answer 'yes' or 'no' to the following
questions to find out if you're telepathic:

1. Are you bright, bubbly and do you like being the centre of attention at parties?

2. Do you take risks with money, career and love and perhaps enjoy the thrill of a bet?

3. Are you very sensitive and easily hurt by what people say to you?

4. Are you creative? Perhaps you like to paint, write or play music and always have imaginative ideas?

5. Do you believe that psychic powers are real?

6. Are you so sceptical that you believe that, if tested for telepathy, you would score well below chance?

7. Have you ever worried that someone you know at another location is in danger and this was later proved to be true?

8. Are you intuitive? Do you judge people by first impressions and find out later that your initial gut instinct was correct?

9. Do you sometimes know who is calling before you answer the phone?

10. Do pets respond to your feelings or know when you're coming home?

How did you score?
Score 3 points for every 'yes' and 2 for every 'no'. Then add them up.

20–23 Your skull is like a wall of stone. There is no way that telepathic thoughts can get in and out of your head.

24–27 Not bad. You could improve your telepathic powers with a little effort.

28–30 Liars beware – you can read people like a book!

Finally, telepathy can be particularly useful at times of crisis. Many people have spoken to me about how they have known that someone they love is in danger or have altered their plans because they correctly sensed that someone meant them harm. I was personally involved in a minor car accident and my wife knew what had happened as soon as I walked through the front door. Telepathic thoughts are floating all around us all the time like radio signals that we can tune into. They can give us warnings and insights, express our feelings and even protect us.

TIPS FOR BETTER TELEPATHY IN A CRISIS:
1. Trust your first impressions – your telepathic powers may be warning you that a person is not trustworthy.
2. Record your dreams – they can often contain telepathically transmitted information from people far away. Check if you and your friends have ever shared a dream.
3. Be happy – telepathy works best with cheerful people.
4. Stare at someone – see if they react and realize they are being watched.

(Experiment)

How telepathic are you?

The following experiment is best carried out at a party or gathering of family and friends. Parapsychologists have found that, to get a high score in telepathic tests it is important to be in a cheerful frame of mind, as this seems to increase people's ability to communicate by thought. Involve children in your experiment, as they are often more telepathic than adults. There is nothing demeaning about doing telepathy experiments in a party atmosphere – in fact you will probably get better results than in the top laboratories.

1. Write down the list of subjects printed below on scraps of paper, fold them up and put them in a bag. One person is blindfolded and sits on a chair in the middle of the room. A subject is chosen at random from the bag and passed around so that everyone except the 'receiver' knows what it is.

2. The 'receiver' then expresses the feelings and thoughts that they have about the target subject. The 'senders' must try to get as emotionally involved in the subject as possible, and involve all of the five senses when they transmit their thoughts. For example, supposing you choose the topic 'burning your fingers on a coal fire', you must feel the pain, see the reds and oranges of the fire, feel the movement of the flames, hear the crackling and smell the smoke. The 'receiver' must relax and let their mind become as still as possible. If you are the 'receiver', you should not struggle to guess what the image is, but let your thoughts flow and say immediately what comes into your head, no matter how silly it may sound. You must be completely spontaneous with what you say or your own mind will interfere with the telepathic impressions you receive.

3. Afterwards count up how many of the things said come close to the target response and how many were wrong. You will probably find that the answers you get are more accurate than could ever be achieved by guesswork alone.

Target Subjects
The following will provide a good starting point for your experiment, although of course you can make up your own as well.

Burning your fingers on a coal fire
A wet dog barking.
Falling out of an aeroplane without a parachute.
Running through a forest.
Biting into a lemon.
Walking through snowy mountains.
Water skiing.
Riding a bicycle.
Dancing at a rock concert.
Running though the waves by an exotic beach.

Case File 1

Joan Scowcroft was having breakfast in a restaurant in the quiet village of Holemoor, North Devon, when a very odd-looking man came through the door. She goes on:

His behaviour, posture and facial expression all indicated that he was 'not quite right'. Then he lurched towards me and grabbed my keys. He dashed out of the restaurant and made off towards town.

Fortunately, Joan was immediately able to ring the police and by lunchtime the keys were back in her possession. The police cautioned the man and ordered him to stay away from the village. Joan, a little shaken, returned home to her cottage:

> Despite the reassurances of the police I still felt ill at ease. I kept seeing images in my mind's eye of the man stalking me. It was as if I could sense his thoughts reaching out to me, like the feeling someone was staring at me. Suddenly I was gripped with fear. My cats began to make a pitiful whining sound. 'My God! He's coming to get me!' I said out loud.
>
> I was feeling very nervous and, to take my mind off my worries, I decided to make some changes in the kitchen. To start with, I decided to swap the kitchen knives, which included a dagger-like instrument, from the drawer and replace them with tea towels.
>
> No sooner had I finished when I heard a key turn in the lock and the next moment I was confronted by the madman. He strode into the kitchen and stood beside the drawer that I had just emptied. 'The Lord has ordered me to kill you so that this cottage will become mine,' he bellowed. 'I will make it as quick and clean as I can.' As he spoke, his eyes fixed on me, he opened the drawer... and felt the tea towels.
>
> The next moment he shrieked a string of blasphemy and sacrilege, swore he would never work for the Lord again, and raced from the cottage. I believe that if my cats and I hadn't telepathically pre-empted the madman's intentions, I'd be dead by now.

The police investigation that followed revealed that the man had had another set of keys cut during the short time they were in his possession. Unfortunately, he was never caught. Joan has since sold her house and relocated to a new town.

The description Joan gives of her feelings suggests that telepathy was at work. She had a nagging feeling of fear and sensed that she was being watched. For many people their only experience of telepathy is during a crisis situation or when their lives are in danger. In Joan's case, even the cats knew something was wrong. This case demonstrates how telepathy is an essential part of our ancient survival skills. At times of crisis these latent powers may awaken.

Case File 2

Joan Lodge recalls the following story of the birth of her daughter, Deborah:

> My labour pains started at 1 a.m. but I told my husband not to call my parents as they were probably experiencing a bad night. My father was terminally ill and we were expecting him to pass over at any time. 'We'll let him know when it's all over,' I remember saying.

Joan gave birth to her daughter at 3.02 a.m:

> The next day my husband went to tell my Mum and Dad – and was greeted by my Mum. 'I know,' she said before my husband could speak 'we've got a granddaughter.'
>
> Apparently my father had been sleeping peacefully for once, when he suddenly sat up in bed and shook my mother awake. 'Baby Deborah's coming! She's coming! She's *here*!' exclaimed my Dad. Mum looked at the clock. It was 3.02 a.m.

Deborah, now aged 43, says:

> It's a funny way to choose a name. Grandad held me in his arms just before he died. Mum keeps pointing out how similar I am to him. Apparently I have the same mannerisms and even his turns of phrase. He obviously loved me a great deal and sometimes I feel that his spirit is somehow guiding me.

Distance seems to make no difference for telepathy to work. There was a telepathic empathy between Deborah and her grandfather from the moment she was born and it may still be existing between this world and the next.

Case File 3

Bridgitte Stafford found herself in excruciating pain on the bus on her way back from the shops:

> I found a seat and sat down. The pain seemed to come and go in waves, but in this sorry state, and sometimes writhing in agony, I

managed somehow to struggle home.

Of course, I was worried that there was something seriously wrong with me. As I came through the front door of my home it seemed to be getting worse and worse. I slumped exhausted into an armchair and was about to reach for the phone to call the doctor when I was overwhelmed with a great spasm of pain. It was so bad that I called out.

Unbeknown to Bridgitte, her daughter Nicola was in hospital at that same moment and was having a very difficult birth. Nicola says:

The baby kept crowning and going back. The only option left was a forceps delivery. I had lots of Pethidine but the pain was more than I could take. Suddenly I found myself on the ceiling and looking down at everything that was going on. Then the baby came and the next thing I knew, I was back in bed holding her in my arms.

It was at this point that Bridgitte felt the pain lift from her too:

All of a sudden I felt completely at peace. All the pain had gone as quickly and as unexpectedly as it had started. I felt fine and desperately wanted a cup of tea. At that moment the phone rang. It was my daughter ringing from the hospital, 'Congratulations Mum,' said Nicola in an excited voice, 'you're the first to know. I was rushed in and have just had baby Kristina a few minutes ago.

I'm sure that I shared my daughter's labour pains that day and may have experienced even more pain than she did! I now have nine grand-children, but I'm very close to Kristina. It's always me she calls for if she's ill and I always seem to know if she's troubled.

Nicola often wonders if her mother had somehow shared in Kristina's difficult birth. 'We sometimes laugh about it now. When I was out of my body it was like I said, "The pain's too much. Here, Mum – you have it!"'

Scientific experiments may prove that there is a mysterious link between mother and baby. This same telepathic empathy exists between people who care for each other. Nicola's thoughts reached out and linked with her Mum. The powerful psychic bonds that are made at the time of birth may stay with us throughout life. This may explain why telepathy between family members is so often reported.

Telepathy: an ancient skill

I suggested at the beginning of this chapter that telepathy and ESP are ancient survival skills that everybody may have possessed before language was developed. It is not surprising, therefore, to discover that animals, and often family pets, are also psychic. Barbara Woodhouse, the famous television animal trainer, was convinced that mind-to-mind communication takes place between humans and pets:

> I have always been able to understand and read their thoughts. They come on my brain just as if they were speaking my language. It is what we send out to them that matters. It goes out in waves. I feel the waves coming back. I thought everyone could do it. I was quite surprised when I found people did not hear what their dogs were thinking.[1]

Many pet owners believe exactly the same. Jenny Ashwell, a secretary at a vet's surgery, describes her experience:

> I have a Siamese cat called Biscuits, and I'm sure that he's psychic. He miraculously appears at the doorstep the moment I arrive home from work. Even when I arrive early or late he still seems to know when I'll arrive. My son Airrion, who lives with me, has noticed that Biscuits will jump up on the windowsill and look for me if I telephone to say I'm on my way home.

I have noticed similar behaviour in our family pets. Our rabbits seem to obey our mental commands if we will them in from the back garden and through the back door. Our dog, a Jack Russell, escaped from the garden one day when my wife Jane was out visiting a friend's new house three miles away. 'I was amazed when he turned up at my friend's,' says Jane. 'I'd travelled by car, so there is no way I could have left a scent, and William had never been taken to that address before.'

One of the strangest stories of pets finding their masters happened to Private James Brown of the 1st North Staffordshire Regiment, when he was sent to join the Great War in France in August 1914. On the 27 September, his wife wrote to him to break the bad news that Prince, his Irish terrier, was missing. But Prince had already joined his master in the trenches. The dog had somehow travelled over 200 miles through the south of England, crossed the English Channel and then walked another 60 miles of battlefield to his master's frontline position at Armentières.

Scientific research is slowly beginning to substantiate the many anecdotal claims of pet owners who say that their animals are psychic. Psychologist Michael Fox of Washington University studied extraordinary cases of psychic cats. In his book *Understanding your Cat* [2] he records how a New York vet left his pet behind when he was relocated to a new job 2,500 miles away in California. Six months later an identical cat walked into his new home. When he examined it he found a deformation on the fourth vertebra of the tail – an injury he had himself treated when the cat was bitten as a small kitten. With no sensory clues to guide him, how did the cat know where to locate his owner?

Animals who find their owners in this way may be displaying a form of clairvoyance that parapsychologists have called 'remote viewing'. This is the ability to 'see' distant locations without the use of the five senses. During the Cold War the CIA funded psychics to use this technique to spy on Soviet military bases.

In Russia the Soviets had their own X-files, and much of their research into the paranormal was done with animals. According to Sheila Ostrander and Lynn Schroeder in *Psychic Discoveries Behind the Iron Curtain* [3], Dr Pavel Naumov claimed that a series of shockingly cruel tests were undertaken with rabbits to see if telepathy took place between a mother rabbit and her new-born litter. A submarine was commandeered, the baby rabbits taken on board, and the mother rabbit wired up on shore with electrodes to monitor her brain patterns. The baby rabbits were then killed at pre-arranged times and the mother rabbit's brain waves tested. 'At the instant of death, her brain reacted,' says Dr Naumov. 'There *was* communication and our instruments clearly registered these moments of ESP.'

French scientific experiments in 1968 showed that rats could foretell the future. Scientists observed the behaviour of the rats, and then a machine selected a number of them randomly to be put to death. It was noted that the condemned rats had exhibited different behavioural patterns before the machine had made its selection, suggesting that they had some kind of presentiment of their death.

Scientists today, such as Rupert Sheldrake, claim that all living beings have morphogenic fields – invisible vibrations that surround and give shape to life forms, and affect their behaviour. This interconnection of life energy and thought extends across the barriers between species and may even increase the intelligence of animals as a result of contact with their human companions.

Pets have often been known to mimic human behaviour and can sometimes display remarkably intelligent actions. For example, they frequently learn to cope with locks on new refrigerators within minutes of it being installed, so that they can help themselves to food. Parapsychologists have argued that they receive this information from the thoughts of their owners.

Just as we influence our pets, so they in turn influence us. Tests on patients suffering from high blood-pressure reveal that both systolic and diastolic blood-pressure will reduce when a pet is present. Research has also shown that pet-owning cardiac patients live longer than other patients with similar heart conditions.

The father of parapsychology, Joseph Banks Rhine, dedicated his life to the study of ESP and psychic phenomena. He wrote:

> The number of reported cases on animal ESP is large enough to suggest that animals can somehow be affected by circumstances they could not be aware of by any sensory sign and which one would suppose they could hardly understand in human terms.[4]

In other words, there is overwhelming evidence to suggest that animals are psychic.

1. *Psychic News*, 23 July 1988.
2. Published by Random House, New York, 1974.
3. Published by Abacus, London, 1973.
4. *New Frontiers on The Mind*, Pelican, 1937.

Chapter Three
Flights in Time

Most people have experienced that eerie feeling of *déjà vu* (literally 'seen before'), in which a person feels that they have witnessed or experienced a situation before. Sometimes, in the middle of a conversation everything seems to become strangely familiar. It is like watching a film, then suddenly realizing that you have already seen it. Usually the sensation lasts only a few seconds but there are pathological cases on record where the subject has had a prolonged, or even constant, feeling of *déjà vu*. Most people experience the phenomenon occasionally, usually under conditions of fatigue or heightened sensitivity.

Science still can't adequately explain *déjà vu*. One theory says that it is caused when one side of the brain receives messages a fraction of a second after the other. Or it may be that the *déjà vu* experience is a memory mix-up caused when repressed memories surface. Some say that it is simply because the experience reminds you of a real, partly recalled event – like the infuriating act of trying to recall a name that is on the tip of your tongue.

How does science explain the experiences of people such as David Martin, who told me about his *déjà vu* experience in Singapore? While travelling through some unfamiliar terrain in a jeep with his friends he had a profound sense of *déjà vu* and soon realized that he 'knew' the unfamiliar terrain:

> At the cross-roads I said, 'Turn left here, because just down the road is a lovely tea house. It has a large red sign and a large stone dog outside. When we approach a Malaysian girl dressed in black will wave to us.'
>
> Everyone in the car laughed and reminded me that none of us had ever visited the area before. We turned left and there was the tea house exactly as I had described it with the red sign, stone dog and the Malaysian girl standing outside waving to us.

David's *déjà vu*, like thousands of similar reports, included information about the future – a future that was to unfold only moments after
he had made his prediction. Many other people have told me how
they have seen back through time and witnessed events from the past.
These spontaneous uncalled-for glimpses may explain some of the
strange, yet consistent, accounts of ghostly sightings. For example,
John Slade and his wife Elsie spoke of their strange experience in Sri
Lanka:

> To get to our hotel in time we were forced to cut across the railway
> line. The old steam trains normally made quite a racket – you could
> hear them hissing and clanking from miles away. I noticed a bright
> light behind us. Assuming that a train was coming, I quickly pulled
> my wife away from the rails as a large train brushed by, almost
> touching us.
>
> Even though it was an old steam train it was totally silent – not just
> quiet, it was *totally* silent. The steam, the wheels, the carriages made
> not a single sound. We were so close that we could also see that the
> train had no driver, no passengers and no guard.
>
> I'm a sceptical man – I was trained in the navy and have worked as
> a councillor – so I went next morning to ask the stationmaster about
> the incident. He insisted that no trains passed that way at the time I
> said, and he added we were not the first to see a strange train at this
> track. Where we had walked had been the site of a number of fatal
> train disasters!

John and Elsie believed that they had seen a ghost train. Or did they
experience a time slip and witness a scene from the past? Is it possible
for ordinary people, who make no claim to psychic powers, to 'see'
both the past and future?

Psychologist Dr Keith Hearne is a member of the Society for Psychical Research and heads the BBC's prediction bureaux for the
programme *Out of this World*. He explains:

> Premonition exists – even though it defies the known laws of the
> universe. Everything in the universe may happen all at once and our
> lifetime is but one segment of this wholeness. I predict that one of the
> most important questions for the science of the next millennium will
> be concerned with the illusion of time.

It could be that precognition is an ancient instinctive warning signal,
and this may explain why it is threatening events in the future that

are the most easily perceived. For some people unwanted visions of the future can be very worrying. Mrs Feist had the following experience:

> I kept having terrible repetitive nightmares of a nuclear disaster by a tall tower. I would thrash in my sleep and was heard to call out, 'The Russians! The Russians!' The meaning of my nightmares was revealed on television some weeks later. I saw on the news a picture of the very tower that I had just been dreaming about: the Chernobyl power station in Russia.

One of the most chilling stories of precognition was sent to me by Mr Lizakowski of West Yorkshire:

> In the early 1960s I attended Cottingley Manor School and I remember how one day in the school playground a boy was describing a dream to every boy or girl present there.
>
> 'Peter will commit murder,' he said convincingly. 'And it will be horrible! Horrible! Horrible!' In distressed tones he said the words over and over again.

Nobody believed the boy's terrible prophesy about their classmate – who many years later was to become the notorious British serial killer Peter Sutcliffe.

Seeing through time

Over the years I have trained many people to unlock their powers of prophesy. At first my students believe that they have no special powers, but with a little practice they quickly obtain sometimes quite startling results.

The most important key to predictive power is to *believe in yourself!* Trust your intuitive insight. Don't censor your thoughts. Allow your intuition to tell you what it already knows. You can see through time and soon you are going to prove it. With a little help and some deliberate experimentation you will see how easy it is to trigger these extraordinary powers. First, you need to ask yourself the questions listed below. If you can answer 'yes' to most or all of them you are already a long way down the path to seership. Afterwards try the simple experiment (see p.56) to test just how accurate your powers to see through time are.

Quiz

Do you have the power of prophesy?

Answer 'yes' or 'no' to the following questions:

1. Have you ever dreamed of an event that has then happened?

2. When visiting a strange place, have you had a sense that you have been there before?

3. Have you ever applied for a job and known you were going to get it even though the odds were stacked against you?

4. Have you ever known that, despite their abilities, some child-hood friends would do well in life and others fail?

5. Do you ever know what somebody is going to be wearing before you meet them?

6. Have you ever cancelled a journey because of a gut feeling that something bad was going to happen?

7. When playing card games have you ever anticipated which card will be drawn next?

8. Have the news headlines ever reflected your own misgivings about what was going to happen?

9. Are you lucky with the National Lottery?

10. Have you ever felt that a friend will unexpectedly get into trouble and they do?

How did you score?

If you answered 'no' to every question, you have a long way to go before being able to see the future. In fact, you may never experience precognitive thoughts because you are resisting them.

If you answered 'yes' to one to four questions, you have an average precognition ability. Given time, you could develop it.

If you answered 'yes' to between five and eight questions, you really do have a gift. Your mind is definitely receptive to future events.

If you answered 'yes' to between eight and ten questions, you are a regular Madam Za Za and can see the future – but then you probably know that already!

Can you 'see' the past?

Many psychics and mediums believe that a stream of vibration emanates from everyone and is absorbed into the environment. When you visit an ancient building, such as a cathedral, you may become aware of these vibrations and sense this as an 'atmosphere'. You can feel the holiness and peace of the place in your bones.

Most people employ this sensitivity to the past when they buy a home. A place has to 'feel right' before you buy it. A gut feeling tells you whether it feels like home or has a bad atmosphere. You are reading the positive and negative vibrations of events that have taken place in there.

In the same way vibrations can be absorbed into objects like jewellery or a watch, and these can be unlocked by a psychic technique called psychometry. An object held in the hand contains the whole history of events that once took place around it. Try the following experiment to test your psychometric powers.

1. Ask a friend to lend you a small object, such as a watch or ring, that belongs to someone they know. The history of the object should be known by your friend but not by you. You are going to describe the life and character of the object's owner.

2. Close your eyes, relax and allow your intuitive thinking to flow. Believe in yourself – don't worry about making mistakes. Say exactly what comes to you and don't censor or interpret the images that you see. What is the first thing you feel? Is this a warm person or a cold, insensitive person? Is this person a worrier? Are they happy or sad? Shy or outgoing?

3. Now dig deeper. Describe any scenes and pictures that come to mind. Can you describe their childhood? What significant events have happened in their life? What countries have they visited? Do any other locations come to mind? In short, describe a brief history of their life. Let it flow. But don't make predictions. Psychometry is all about reading the past.

4. When you dry up, ask your friend to tell you what percentage you got right. Ask them also about specific things you may have said. Psychometry is a psychic ability that most people can develop with practice and you may really surprise yourself with your accuracy!

Retrocognition

Many ordinary people claim to have had spontaneous glimpses of the past. For some it is more than sensing an atmosphere, they see a whole series of events unfold just as if they are experiencing these things first-hand. It may be that they glimpse into some other level of reality that is beyond time and space as we understand it. In the letters I have received from people who have had these experiences, their descriptions are extremely vivid. The case files that follow have been abridged, but the details reveal much about the writers' reactions. Often they are puzzled or frightened by what has happened, and it is clear that these bizarre stories have not been made up, but I'll leave it up to you to decide whether these people really are time-travellers or whether they have been tricked somehow by their unconscious.

Case File 1

Beverley was looking around a local market with her husband, when the following strange events took place:

> As we looked around the market my husband said to me, 'I've just seen a lovely dinner service on a stand near the shop over there. If we're quick we may just be able to buy it in time.' As we rushed over to the stall, he told me that a strange old lady with long grey hair tied back ran it. The stall had the oddest collection of things for sale – most of them from the 1950s.
>
> But when we got to the stall it was completely empty. Only seconds ago it had been full of wares. Perplexed by what had happened, my husband asked a man, who was sitting nearby selling his paintings, if he had seen the old lady and her stall. 'I couldn't understand why you were looking at an empty stall,' said the man. 'And who were you talking to?'
>
> Further enquiries revealed that the site of the stall was once owned by a little old lady with distinctive long grey hair. She had stopped trading in the 1950s. Did my husband have a vision of the past?

Beverley's case is typical of the letters sent to me on this intriguing subject of looking back in time. Of course her husband may have seen a ghost, but it is more likely that he experienced a 'time slip'. This may sound like science fiction, but there are many other well-authenticated examples. For example, some visitors to the palace of Versailles near Paris have suddenly found themselves transported to the time of Marie Antoinette. Remarkably, the scenes these psychic time-travellers have described have been checked and proved to be historically accurate. The details described by them about the palace's layout are known only to the most knowledgeable historians. Another explanation may be that these are not 'time slips', but unconscious memories of past lives (see p.141 ff.).

Case File 2

Len Rodney's story raises many questions. Did he experience a time slip, clairvoyance, or precognition? Or was it some kind of indication that he had once lived in Russia centuries ago? How would you react if this happened to you?

> While sightseeing in Russia fourteen years ago, I came across a large ornamental monument in a public garden. As soon as I set eyes on it I had a strange feeling that I had seen it before. I stood for some time before I remembered. I had dreamed about it in every detail: the black and white marble squares, the little arched wooden door at the top flanked by two colourful dragons that spouted water from their mouths to the row of white marble statues on either side of the monument.
>
> In my dream I slid down the tiles and past the dragons. I wondered if I had lived there in a past life and slid down those familiar banisters as a child? How on earth could I have dreamed in such detail of a place where I have never been before?

Certain places give me an eerie feeling also, as if I've known the place before but can't explain how or when. Perhaps this is caused by dim memories of past lives, which are trying to reawaken since we crossed the river of forgetting. Or maybe we are picking up vibrations left recorded in the environment. Whatever the explanation an experience of this sort can shake even the most courageous of men, as the following case file shows.

Case File 3

Harry MacMillan of Edinburgh was working for the fire brigade when the following events took place:

We were called to extinguish a fire at an old stone building that had long ago been used as a lodging house. When we returned to the station we realized that we had left behind a shovel, so I returned alone to get it.

As I stood in the silent, smouldering building I noticed an old wooden structure that must have been the serving area, where the owner would have allocated the beds for the night. Suddenly I was transported back in time and actually saw the lines of flotsam and jetsam queuing up. I also heard many different dialects being spoken. Soon I became aware of the drudgery that these poor people lived with and sensed their presence all around me and felt a great sadness for these ghostly figures. The scene so engrossed me that I couldn't even remember picking up the shovel that was now in my hand. This vision of despair was so powerful that it has stayed with me all of my life. I believe that somehow I had seen through time and I still shudder when I think of it.

Harry's experience reminds me of a well-known story from the west country. In 1936, sixteen-year-old Stephen Jenkins was exploring in Looe Bar in Cornwall, where King Arthur is said to have met his death. He was astonished to see a host of medieval warriors in chain mail appear before him. Thirty-eight years later he returned to the same spot with his wife and the same vision reappeared to both of them.

Some people claim that places such as Looe Bar are situated on the intersection of ley lines and are places of great psychic power. Ley lines are lines of natural energy that allegedly run through the earth and connect ancient monuments. In particular, the energy is icreased at places where two ley lines cross each other. Perhaps the building that Harry MacMillan visited was also a place of great psychic energy.

I have received letters from many Scottish people, and I am convinced that they are a very special people with a unique psychic heritage that stretches back way before the times of the Celts. Many great mediums were Scots, and many of my most interesting letters have come from ordinary people in Scotland. The following is one of my favourites.

Case File 4

Ernest Rowe of Glasgow takes us back to the early history of Scotland when witches, elves and fairies roamed the land:

In 1966 my wife and I decided to holiday at the Isle of Skye. It was a late evening in August when we approached the bridge near Dunvegan. We came across an enormous number of cats. They were everywhere and some were even jumping onto the bonnet of our van. I have never seen so many cats gathered together at one time; the road, the bridge, everywhere was swarming with them. I said to my wife, 'We are surely reaching civilization as there are plenty of cats around!' Later we stopped at the local inn and asked about the bridge. The landlord told us that it was nicknamed the Fairy Bridge and also known as the Bridge of Cats. Not many of the locals own cats today, but years ago the bridge was the haunt of a witch. What we saw has been described by many a frightened traveller. Legend says that the mystical bridge is haunted by the spirits of the witch's cats!

All these case files suggest that it is possible for ordinary people to have glimpses of history. However, I receive far more reports of people's glimpses of the future. Of course, Jane's and my own work often involves prophesy and seership, and in a great many cases we have predicted the future with startling accuracy.

The gift of prophesy is much more widespread than you may expect. The following case files are told by ordinary people who make no claim to having special powers. They form just a small selection from a huge mailbag that I have received on this subject. At the end of the chapter (see p.66) I have included a simple experiment for you to try, to see if you too have the power to see into the future.

Case File 5

Jennifer T. relates the following experience:

Soon after my father died I had an early-morning dream about him. He joked, as he had done in life, had a silver light around him and when he reached out and touched my hands he felt warm and normal. 'It's true! There is an afterlife!' I exclaimed in my dream. 'Have you met Aunty Alice and Grandma Coates?' I asked. 'Of course I have,' replied my father, 'but there's something very important that I must tell you. Mum is not well; she must attend to her chest.'

I had to wait until Mum returned from holiday before I could tell her about the dream. 'I'm fine,' she said, 'there's nothing wrong with me.' But I persisted when I noticed a nasty red lump on her chest. I insisted that she visit the doctor to get it checked.

The lump was cancerous. Mum had radiation treatment at St Mary's hospital and the cancer was caught just in time. She is now 90 years old and as fit as a fiddle.

Dreams that happen in the early-morning dream phase are often the most vivid. At these times some people have 'lucid dreams' which are as clear as waking awareness. It could be argued that Jennifer's subconscious mind may have already observed her mother's red lump and told her about it in a dream. But I believe the simpler answer: the spirit of Jennifer's father communicated to save her mother's life. Communication with the afterlife can sometimes be very useful, and in this case it helped with the future. I've discovered in the course of my work that when I make a prediction given to me by the spirit world it is invariably right. The spirit communicators try to give helpful information that will guide their loved-ones here on earth to make the best decisions.

Case File 6

Mediums are not in the prediction business, but any information that is given to them by the spirit world about the future is guided by the love of those the sitter knows on the other side. Psychic predictions are not protected in this way and not usually as accurate as those that come via mediumship, although even amateur psychics are sometimes right.

Untrained psychic powers can cause upset, and I know of many professional psychics who make very frightening predictions for people. Elsie had one such experience:

I called in on my best friend for a cup of coffee and a chat. As I carried the empty cups out to the kitchen for her she said with a startled tone, 'I have just seen a funeral cortege follow you into the kitchen, but there's no coffin, just mourners carrying wreaths at their sides!' 'Oh dear,' I replied, and left it at that.

The next day my husband, whom we assumed was perfectly fit, had a massive heart attack and died. Ten years before he had made arrangements for his body to be donated to science which meant that no coffin was needed. A memorial service was held and as the premonition had predicted, there was a line of mourners carrying wreaths but no coffin.

Unfortunately, spontaneous, uncontrolled clairvoyance usually reveals negative things. Dreams are also a rich source of precognitive material, but again tend to be uncontrolled. Often the unconscious will tell you the gist of what is going to happen, but it misses out essential components. Dreams speak to us in symbols, puns, metaphors and allegories and they use these same methods when they tell us about the future as the next case study, about a woman writing under the initials R.D. reveals:

> I awoke from a vivid dream and told it to my husband so that I could put it into my diary later. The dream was not pictorial, it was auditory. I had heard a name, 'Neville' – not that unusual, but I didn't know anyone by that name. I had also dreamed of the poem 'Upon West-minster Bridge' by the poet William Wordsworth.
>
> Three months later I joined a discussion group and was introduced to a Neville Westbridge. We became good friends and his ideas have had a very important influence on my philosophy of life. My husband has always been very sceptical about precognition but the accuracy of this dream has made him change his tune.

I am always pleased to hear from those of the older generation who often come forward with some amazing psychic stories to tell. This is mainly because they have had a lot more experience, have often known the tragedy of bereavement, and have devoted time in their later years reflecting upon the meaning of life and what follows after death. I particularly enjoy hearing of how psychic powers played a part in the lives of the people who lived through the war. This story comes from a man writing under the name of Sydney B.:

> At nine years of age I read a story book called *Poland – Land of the Rainbow*. I was transfixed and my imagination roamed the country as if I was actually there. For years afterwards the same strange name 'Posen' kept coming to my mind. I often heard the words 'Posen, Posen, Posen' being called out to me. I heard it in my mind but it was as clear as a real voice.
>
> During the war I fought in Norway but was captured in 1940 and spent five years in various POW camps. In 1945 I was on the 1,000-

mile death march from Poland through Czechoslovakia to Moosburgh Stalag 7A near Munich. During my imprisonment the Germans put us on a train to do a propaganda march around a town. The town's name was Posen.

From Posen we were taken to a nearby camp called Fort Winiary. I befriended a Polish girl in the kitchens who would give us extra food. One day she was able to get us an English book. I couldn't believe my eyes when she gave it to me: *Poland – Land of the Rainbow*, the very book that had triggered my obsession with Posen all those years ago!

Even as a child of nine something told Sydney that Posen would have a monumental impact upon his life, almost as if his future was already planned. I have always believed that we have free will, and that we are given glimpses of the future so that we can avoid an adverse destiny. From an evolutionary point of view this makes sense, as it would help the survival of our species. Whether there is free will or an unalterable destiny will always be a subject of debate and perhaps we will never know the answer for certain. The next two case files are interesting examples of this dichotomy.

Case File 9

Joan M. relates the following story:

A couple of months ago, my husband woke up and told me that an old Red Indian told him that esha ness meant the 'eye of the storm'. My husband guessed that Esha Ness was a race horse so we scanned the papers for days to see if it was running. We'd almost forgotten about the dream, when we discovered Esha Ness was running in the Grand National – so naturally we backed it. We stood to win almost £5,000 but that was the year that the Grand National was abandoned because of a false starting signal. Some of the horses ran, unaware of the mix-up, and even though Esha Ness won, we lost out.

My husband firmly believes that because he backed the horse, things happened the way they did. Can a person control fate in this way or is this just a bizarre coincidence?

Many psychic people have spirit guides from the North American Indian tradition, and Joan's husband's guide may have been proving his reality by giving him the winner of the Grand National. I have certainly found that my own spirit guides can play tricks in this way. For example, I can sometimes stand in front of an audience and tell a string of people what six numbers they choose every week for the lottery. The odds for doing this are, of course, millions to one. But can I predict the numbers for next week? No, not a single one. It can be very infuriating, but I think that this says something about the nature of spiritual gifts: they cannot be used solely for material gain.

(Case File 10)

This story from Dolores G. may be proof that psychic powers cannot be used to win money:

> I dreamed I was looking at a pools coupon and saying to my daughter, 'Oohh, look at the strange way the draws have come up. They're all at the bottom of the form!' I told my daughter about the dream but nonetheless did my usual numbers that week. Then, yes you guessed it, the result was that there were 11 draws in the last 12 entries. I was upset, of course, but not for long. Two weeks later my regular numbers came up and I won £1,510! I believe that despite not following my dream I was meant to win.

Maybe if Dolores had paid attention to her dream she could have won the pools twice! We may never unravel all these mysteries of destiny.

Prediction

Of course, prediction is one of the areas that newspapers are eager to tap into, although this is not the most important part of Jane's and my work. When Princess Diana met Dodi Fayed, the *Sunday Mirror* asked me to make some predictions about what would happen. I told the journalist the various things that came to me but added that it was possible that none of them would happen because I felt that Prince Charles was going to be involved in a serious car accident that would change the course of events. The journalist said that she couldn't print this, and I got it wrong. A car accident did of course change the course of events, but I had seen the wrong person.

Case File 11

Prediction, and indeed all the psychic gifts, are so easily misseen or misheard. Here is an excellent example of this, sent to me by a Mr D., that shows just how subtle clairvoyance can be:

> I often have premonitions about events that I read about later in the paper. The most disturbing experience happened recently and while I was wide awake. All day long I kept hearing in my head, 'The Queen is dead. Long live the King!' It ran over and over in my thoughts like a catchy song that you can't get out of your mind. I was beginning to wonder if the Queen was going to die.
>
> The next day it was announced that Diana had died in a car crash. Across Kensington Palace was soon draped a banner saying 'Diana – Queen of Hearts'. The queen had died – but not the one I expected.

Experiment

Dream experiment

There is a state between sleeping and waking that psychologists call hypnagogic dreaming. These 'dreams' are a flow of vivid but brief mental images and can occur just before you fall off to sleep. The images can sometimes possess an overwhelming sense of reality, with much detail and supersaturated colour. Some psychologists have pointed out a similarity between the images seen in a crystal ball and the experience of hypnagogic imagery. And, like the crystal ball, hypnagogic dreams contain potent omens and visions of the future. Harness their power, and you can use your dreams to see the future. You can become the psychic newscaster.

1. First, choose a target subject to dream about. Select something in which you are interested but not emotionally involved, so that your inner hopes and fears don't influence your insights. For this experiment we will try to dream about next week's main news stories.

2. Put a copy of a newspaper by the side of your bed before retiring. Touch it so that you focus your attention as you prepare to go to sleep. Now ask yourself, 'What important news headlines will be in this paper over the coming week?'

3. As you drop off to sleep you will try to stimulate hypnagogic mental imagery and manipulate the visions. To stimulate this awareness it is important to completely relax, but don't let yourself fall asleep straight away. The secret of hypnagogic dreaming is to hold your awareness between waking and the onset of sleep.

4. As you teeter on the brink of sleep watch your thoughts, but don't follow them. Be the observer of yourself. Instead of thinking in words, try to think in pictures. For example, you think, 'I ought to do the gardening tomorrow'. Convert this into a picture – see the garden, the flowers, the sky. Gradually you'll stimulate a flow of visual imagery. Many scenes and pictures will flash before your mind's eye.

5. Now imagine a blank copy of the newspaper is in front of you. Next, transfer the stream of imagery onto the white pages. By linking the images you are encouraging your subconscious mind to associate the images it throws up with the future headlines. You trigger your precognition.

6. Then imagine the images changing to printed words. Try to read them. At first you may just pick up one or two words. You may only see 'Politician', but the next day you read, 'Politician in sex scandal with vicar'. Now pull yourself back from your reverie and frantically write down your predictions before they fade.

7. If you see nothing, let go, drop off to sleep and instead write your dream down in the morning. By programming yourself to dream of future events you most probably will. You may find an accurate prediction of future events is contained in next morning's dream in symbolic form.

Chapter Four
Strange Coincidences

A dinner on 25 July 1884 will always be remembered in our family because of the unusual main course: my great-grandfather's cousin, a 17 year-old cabin boy called Richard Parker.

Our family roots are in Woolston on Southampton Water, and, like many of my family before and after him, Richard ran away to sea. He boarded the *Mignonette*, a ship built on the Thames for an Australian millionaire who wanted to explore the Great Barrier Reef. The captain of the vessel, Thomas Dudley, had trouble commissioning a crew for her long maiden voyage, so to avoid delay her owner went on ahead by ocean liner. Later the *Mignonette*, with Edwin Stephens as mate and Edmund Brooks as hand, left Southampton, their last port-of-call, for the long haul to Australia.

It was Parker's first voyage on the high seas. Captain Dudley was a sturdy and resourceful captain, and Stephens and Brooks went about their duties efficiently, but Parker had problems. Dudley wrote in his log: 'June 28th. Break in the weather. First heavy seas. Yawl sound and handles well. Cabin boy a poor sailor.'

They were 1,600 miles from land when the South Atlantic hurricane broke. The *Mignonette* was hit by huge waves and sank in five minutes. The captain's log records: 'July 5th. Hit by hurricane on port beam. Mast away, sails torn. Enormous seas. *Mignonette* sinks. Take to open dinghy. Very little food.'

In the panic to board the lifeboats, Parker threw their water barrel and provisions into the sea expecting them to float – but they sank. Dudley bravely climbed aboard the wreck to see what else could be salvaged, but all he managed to grab were two tins of turnips which he mistook for meat. The turnips did not last long between four people and survival was looking less and less likely. They caught a splash of rainwater in a cape and Dudley, using a clasp knife tied to an oar, was able to kill a turtle. The knife was to come in useful again later.

They were drifting from the shipping lanes, pushed onward by violent storms. Parker began to drink sea water. The captain wrote: 'July 16th. No sight of shipping. Estimate at least seven more days with contrary winds. Parker sick. Sea water. Turtle hard to digest. Raw and oily.'

Parker was becoming weak and delirious with thirst and, much of the time, was in a semi-conscious state. The others were exhausted, weary and desperate, but determined to survive as long as possible. However, the ordeal was becoming too much for the cabin boy: his pale, gaunt body shook with the effects of dehydration, his mind raced with thoughts of home and hatred for his first sea voyage. Captain Dudley did his best to keep up morale: 'July 23rd. Parker delirious. Must have drunk more sea water. Crew in poor spirits – nerves frayed. Need food desperately.'

Stories about cannibalism at sea were familiar to these men. Some seamen argued that it was defensible in extreme conditions; and there were many songs, sea shanties and poems which developed the theme. Dudley considered drawing lots to decide which of them should die to save the others, but then Parker took a turn for the worse. They had been adrift now for 16 days with no sign of land: 'July 24th. Have finally reached a decision. The three of us have decided that the boy must die.'

Dudley persuaded Stephens and Brooks that the boy lying desperately ill at the bottom of the boat should be sacrificed for the survival of them all. It must have been an agonising debate, particularly for Dudley, who was known as a man of exemplary character. Brooks was the hardest to convince and baulked when it came to the moment for action. He went as far away as possible while Dudley and Stephens said some prayers over Parker's sleeping body. Then, Dudley shook the lad by the shoulder and said: 'Wake up, Dick my boy, your time has come.' Stephens held the boy's legs. They cut his throat and caught the streaming blood in a rusty bailer. The two men, dying of dehydration and half-mad with fear and doubt, drank the warm blood. Dudley dissected the bleeding corpse with his clasp knife. Even Brooks, his body tormented with thirst and hunger, joined in the grisly meal. (It is said that human flesh tastes like sweet pork.) At his trial, Dudley wept:

> I offered up a prayer most fervently that God might forgive us for such an act. It was my decision to take the boy's life, but it was justified by an overriding necessity. As a result I have lost only one member of my crew in circumstances in which all would otherwise have perished.

The meal kept them alive until 29 July when they were sighted by the *SS Montezuma* – an aptly named vessel, as Montezuma was the Aztec king who, to the horror of the bloodthirsty Spanish conquistador Cortés, ate the flesh of sacrificed children. Captain Dudley and his remaining crew made no attempt to hide the dismembered corpse of the sacrificed teenager as the ship approached. The *Montezuma's* German captain had Richard Parker's remains buried at sea. Dudley, Stephens and Brooks did not try to hide the shame of their desperate act of survival. Soon after the ship docked in the Cornish port of Falmouth, they were arrested and stood trial at Exeter Assizes, in Devon, with Brooks as the chief prosecution witness. All three men broke down and cried under cross-examination.

The Victorian public were shocked by the ghastly events which were reported in *The Times*, but were surprisingly sympathetic. Generally, the three accused were cheered on. Judge Baron Huddleston was impressed by Dudley's character and sterling courage.

The legal position was contradictory: on the one hand the men had committed an act of murder, yet if a situation arises where a man is faced with the necessity to kill in order to survive, the law states that he is innocent of murder so long as he has the victim's consent. Many other legal points also challenged the men's guilt, but one of the conclusions was that the killing was premeditated and therefore unjustified in English law. The jury's conclusion was unprecedented, since it expressed its ignorance of whether the men were guilty of murder. In the end it decided that indeed they were and the death sentence was passed, with a recommendation to mercy.

There was an immediate appeal and a retrial using a classic defence, duress of circumstances, which is still quoted in courts today. The seamen were found guilty of manslaughter, and were sentenced to six months' hard labour, after which they disappeared from the public view. It was rumoured that the experience caused Stephens to go mad and that Brooks too suffered and spent his life in mental turmoil. Dudley fled to Australia to start a new life as a ship's chandler. He is also said to have secretly sent money to support Parker's sister through school, before dying of bubonic plague.

The story has a strange twist in its tail. Half a century before these grisly events took place, Edgar Allen Poe wrote in 1837 *The Narrative of Arthur Gordon Pym of Nantucket*. This short story tells of four shipwrecked men who, after many days' privation, drew lots to decide who should be killed and eaten. The cabin boy drew the short straw. His name was Richard Parker:

He made no resistance whatever and fell instantly dead when stabbed in the back by Peters.... Having in some measure appeased the raging thirst which consumed us by drinking the blood of the victim, and having by common consent taken off the hands, feet and head, and throwing them, together with the entrails, into the sea, we devoured the rest of the body, piecemeal....

The case continues

My cousin Nigel Parker was the first to notice the link between the Poe story and the later real events and wrote about it in a letter to *The Sunday Times* (5 May 1974). The author of a book about strange coincidences told me that some time after *The Sunday Times* letter had been published, he casually mentioned it to a colleague at the University of Edinburgh, who had, that day, written about it in his journal.

Nigel's father, Keith, thought that Richard's story would make an interesting theme for a radio play and began to plan a synopsis. At that time, to supplement his writer's income, he reviewed books for Macmillan publishers. The first book to arrive through the post was entitled *The Sinking of the Mignonette*. A few weeks later he was asked to review another play, among a collection of short plays, called *The Raft*. It was a comedy for children with nothing sinister about it at all, apart from the cover illustration which showed three men apparently threatening a young boy. The illustration is completely out of keeping with the play's tone. *The Raft* was written by someone called Richard Parker.

In the summer of 1993, my parents took in three Spanish students. My father told them about Richard Parker one evening over supper (probably in an attempt to keep the food bills down). The television was on in the background. All conversation stopped when a local programme started talking about the remarkable story. Dad went on to break the silence by saying that weird coincidences always occur whenever Richard's tale is mentioned. He then told them about the Edgar Allen Poe short story.

All three girls went white. 'Look what I bought today,' said one. She reached into her bag and pulled out a copy of *The Narrative of Arthur Gordon Pym of Nantucket*. 'So have I!' said the other two girls in unison. They had all gone shopping independently that day, yet all three girls had bought the very same book containing the Richard Parker story.

Although Parker's body was buried at sea, a headstone was erected in his memory at Pear Tree Churchyard near his birthplace in Woolston, Southampton. The memorial only hints at the tragic story that surrounds his death:

> Sacred to the memory of Richard Parker, aged 17, who died at sea, July 25th 1884, after nineteen days dreadful suffering in an open boat in the tropics, having been wrecked in the yacht *Mignonette*.

> 'Though He slay me yet will I trust in Him.' Job XIII: 15
> 'Lord, lay not this sin to their charge.' Acts VII: 60

My grandfather told of a local family who were paid by the captain to keep the stone clean in perpetuity. They were so ashamed of accepting his money that they asked for their name to be kept secret and they would only clean the stone in the dead of night. In the 1930s it was easily recognized as the brightest stone in the churchyard. In recent decades the gravestone was neglected, but was restored recently with a grant of £350 from Southampton City Council.

I published the Richard Parker story in *The Fortean Times* (Issue 92, November 1996) and it was later covered by the *Sunday Telegraph*. Being aware that strange 'Richard Parker coincidences' often happen to anyone who reads about the story, I invited readers to write to me if anything weird happened to them. It wasn't long before the coincidences started to happen. The first happened on the day I bought *The Fortean Times* to read my article. I had it with me when I went round to my brother Ian's house. There I met my cousin Angela and her then boyfriend who was studying to be a lawyer. 'As a would-be lawyer you'll be interested by my latest article,' I said, passing the magazine to him. After reading the story, he took me over to my brother's dining-room table where he'd been doing his studies. There on the table was the book *Cannibalism and the Common Man* open on the page concerning the case: he had been reading about Judge Baron Huddleston's decision concerning the cannibalism of Richard Parker by Dudley and Stephens.

Other readers of my article reported similar strange coincidences. Janice Robertson wrote to say:

> My husband and I were on holiday in Guernsey staying in the Duke of Normandie Hotel in St Peter Port. As I read your article I was sitting at a table in the bar and on this table is carved the story of the shipwreck and fate of the same cabin boy. I was quite sceptical about this story and could hardly believe it when I saw it in both places.

Joyce Robinson had a similar experience, saying that she read the story in the *Sunday Telegraph,* then again later that same morning in a book called *The Blue Bays of Cornwall.* Also Jo Chipperfield read the story in a newspaper and then moments later by pure chance read about the story again in an obscure book called *Fishy Yarns.*

Some readers also rang me to tell about their weird experiences connected with reading this story. James Plaskett told me of how a family in Hascombe Godalming which had bought the oak door of the prison cell that had closed on Dudley and Stephens. He also said that there were two other Richard Parkers who had brought bad luck at sea. One was hung as the leader of the *Nore* mutiny in 1797, while another died when the *Francis Speight* floundered in 1846. On board a number of seamen had been eaten. He had also experienced a similar coincidence to other people who had read about the story twice in the same day. 'I expect something strange will happen soon,' I said. And it did within seconds. We soon realized that we were both sitting in front of our computer screens, which is not unusual, but were both playing computer chess. I very rarely do this during the day but I needed a break from writing. James Plaskett is a chess grand master.

The strangest coincidence was sent to me by Carlton Morgan:

> After reading the article I received a telephone call from a friend, asking me to help him compose a letter to his employer, Mr Dudley, with whom he was in a legal dispute. We took the letter to a local advice centre to check our legal position.
>
> During the course of the interview my pal was told that Dudley was disregarding acceptable legal procedures. Then we went for coffee, and a discussion over the mindset of the boss class ensued. 'Well, I reckon this riding roughshod over legal procedures is in his blood,' said my friend. 'This guy is into tracing his ancestors, and one of them was a sea captain who was done for eating cabin boy Richard Parker without drawing lots...'

Coincidence and synchronicity

A brave attempt to link coincidence, ESP, and frontier physics was made by the psychical researcher Arthur Koestler (1905–83). He suggested that there is a fundamental law that governs all these three subjects, which, as yet, we do not know. Even the great mind of Koestler was perplexed and he admits in his book *The Roots of*

Coincidence (Random House, New York, 1972) that his theories are only a first step in a darkened room.

It will probably be a physicist or cosmologist who will come up with a plausible theory to explain coincidence. In the strange world of fundamental particles scientists have found that, in certain cases, the laws of causality (the law that cause precedes effect) seems not to apply. For example, some sub-atomic particles like quarks and leptons can exist in more than one place at the same time, arriving before they set off.

Physicists talk about the 'uncertainty principle', which in simple terms means that, according to quantum theory, an electron or any other particle in its natural state has no specific identity or agenda. It has only a potential existence as an aspect of what is called a wave function. When something intrudes on this condition, such as the physicist's experiment, the wave collapses and the electron appears as one of its possible states of size, energy or time. In other words, the material world is not as concrete as we think. It is full of paradoxes, the most intriguing of which is time.

A strange incident involved with time happened to actor Anthony Hopkins when he visited Vienna in 1973 to discuss his new film *The Girl from Petrovka* that was based on a book by author George Feifer. Unfortunately Feifer's original copy containing his important margin notes had been stolen from his car two years earlier in London. The important creative notes that would have been useful for the film would have to be done again.

Coincidence came to their rescue, however. Soon after signing the contract for his film role, Hopkins scoured London for a copy of *The Girl from Petrovka*. He couldn't find a shop that stocked it, and so headed home. On his way home Hopkins noticed an open parcel by his seat in London's Leicester Square underground station. It was a copy of the novel he was looking for. Hopkins handed it to Feifer – it was Feifer's original copy, complete with the margin notes, stolen some two years earlier!

Did Hopkins' desire to find a copy of *The Girl from Petrovka* somehow influence events to attract the book to him? It may be that meaningful coincidences happen because of the influence our unconscious mind has upon the environment. Or perhaps the world that we see outside of ourselves and the world within our head are one and the same. Carl Jung proposed that psychological events corresponded with, and perhaps influenced, physical events. He called this the 'unexpected parallelism between psychic and physical events'. He called his theory synchronicity. By this he meant meaningful coincidence: two events which occur at the same time, and are relevant to one another, but which take place independently (a literal definition of the word *synchronicity* is 'at the same time'.) Time, argued Jung, was more like a web than a straight line of cause and effect. He said: 'Anything done at a particular moment of time has the qualities of that moment in time.' [1]

This is why fortune-telling works. When a psychic casts the Tarot cards, rune stones or throws dice the coincidental fall of the cards, stones or dice is interpreted as an accurate indication of the true nature of a situation. Jung himself was particularly interested in the Chinese oracle book called the *I Ching*, which is normally cast by throwing three coins. Together with a natal chart of a horoscope he would use these oracles to diagnose his patients' psychiatric problems.

Jung experienced many meaningful coincidences himself. On one occasion he was helping a patient understand the symbolism of the Egyptian scarab beetle which had featured in the patient's dream. As he did this a large, brightly coloured beetle, similar in appearance to a scarab, flew into the room.

1 *The Interpretation of Nature and the Psyche*, Routledge & Kegan Paul, 1955.

Chapter Five

Encounters with Spirits and Angels

Many sceptics argue that mediums and psychics gather their information by fishing for information or by watching the facial expressions and body language of their sitters. I hope that the following stories will go some way to disprove this. In each case Jane and I have never met any of the people involved prior to their consultation and, as you will see, there is no way we could have cheated by looking up the information in the public record office. Versions of some of the stories that follow have appeared in various magazines and were authenticated by independent journalists.

Case File 1

It was years since 25-year-old Ken Reynolds had ridden a motorcycle, and even then he hardly ever rode as a pillion passenger. But that was the last journey Ken was ever to make. Moments after leaving home, the motorbike that Ken and his friend were riding was involved in a head-on collision. Both were killed. Ken's mother, Pat Reynolds, describes how she felt:

> I can't find words to adequately describe what I felt. One moment Ken was here and in the next he was gone. I felt empty. Worse than empty. It was like having a big dark hole inside of you – but it had jagged edges.

Pat sunk into a dark depression after the loss of her son. She shut herself away from the world, feeling that life wasn't worth living. However, from the day after he died Ken seemed to make his presence known to her:

Strange things started to happen around the house. The lights would start going on and off, Ken's photo kept falling off the mantelpiece and I saw the morning's dishes lift and move by themselves across the kitchen table. I began to feel that Ken was trying to get in touch with me.

I gained a lot of comfort from visiting my local Spiritualist church. I had a number of messages and went to see a medium privately. The medium, Matthew Smith, was even able to tell me his name straight away and told me other details known only to myself.

Pat was beginning to feel comforted, but the gaping hole inside her still wouldn't go away. It was then that Pat met me at a psychic fair:

I sat down for a tarot reading with Craig. But he pushed the cards aside and said that it was more important that he communicate with my son whom he said I'd only recently lost.

Craig described Ken's personality perfectly, and told me how he died and gave me many factual things about him. In particular, I remember Craig saying that the song 'Lemon tree oh so pretty' was significant. We had a lemon tree in the garden when we lived in South Africa.

A little later Pat booked a private consultation with me at her home and away from the clatter of the fair that we both found distracting.

Craig gave me marvellous proof that Ken was all right in his new life. Ken told Craig how his friend Claire had her hair cropped and had now got a new job in Bristol. He extended his love to his friends Jonathan and Colleen. He also told how he had met his Uncle George and grandfather Percy, and how he loved his gardening. Craig said how I'd been told to buy a ruby ring in Ken's memory, and said that he was joking that I hadn't paid enough for it! And he even gave Ken's birthday and said that a new baby would be born on the same date. It happened as he said.

But, apart from the hard facts, it was Craig's description of Ken's personality that was most convincing. He joked and laughed with Ken and exhibited the same dry humour and tongue-in-cheek tone. I remember Craig saying that Ken said, 'I died with my boots on'. When Ken died he was wearing the new boots that he'd only just bought.

Pat's search was still not over. I invited her to join a circle that meets once a week with the objective of communicating with the spirit world and developing the clairvoyant abilities of those who want to progress. Ken was now able to communicate regularly with his mother and could even speak directly to Pat when I was in a deep trance state:

> I still get depressed about Ken when I think of the wasted years and the grandchildren from him that I will never have. I miss his touch and his humour. But at least I know that he's happy where he is. And best of all I can talk to him whenever I want.

Pat's own psychic abilities have now started to flower and her mediumship is developing at a remarkable rate. It seems that her mediumship has helped her, and I know that she in turn will help many other people in their grief.

Case File 2

The following story is similar to Pat's in many ways, telling of another brave woman coping with her worst nightmare come true. Diana Ashton couldn't come to terms with her son's death – until she spoke to him through Jane.

Diana's son, Mark, absolutely loved motorbikes. He also loved life, family, people and owned a pet chinchilla dog and two other dogs. But his real love was motorbikes, and he would spend hours tinkering and fine-tuning his pride and joy.

Diana goes on:

> I'll never forget that night in August 1994. Mark had been helping me decorate before going out to play pool. It was an exciting time as the next day Mark was to sign the agreement for the mortgage on a flat he was to purchase and share with his friend David. Every mother is a little sad when their children finally leave home. He'd be in his flat by the weekend.
>
> As he left, he smiled and said, 'Bye, Mum.' Then he came back into the lounge, kissed me and said, 'I won't say good-bye. I'll see you later.'

Later that evening the police came to the door bearing terrible news. Twenty-four-year-old Mark had been in collision with a car. The accident had killed him instantly:

I sobbed uncontrollably, as my husband Peter tried to console me. I thought the grief would tear me apart but in those first few days I kept going by organizing the funeral. I dressed him myself, putting on his favourite jeans, shirt and blazer. At his side, I put notes that friends and family had written to him, saying their goodbyes. Finally, when it was time to leave, I placed a single red rose in his hands, kissed him tenderly and whispered, 'Goodnight, my darling.'

They say time is a great healer, but as the months passed I couldn't get the image of Mark in his coffin out of my mind. Whenever I talked of Mark's accident and told people that he was on a motorcycle at the time, they seemed to think that it was his fault almost in the belief that all motorcyclists are 'accidents waiting to happen'. And matters were made worse because of the post-mortem and by not knowing when the inquest was to be held and worrying about its outcome. My doctor prescribed me some anti-depressant tablets and I received some professional counselling but that terrible aching pain just wouldn't go away. One of my biggest fears was that Mark's spirit was trapped in some limbo state and that he was unhappy.

I'd spend hours in his room. 'I'm keeping it exactly as he left it,' I sobbed to Peter. Wracked with grief, I'd gaze at his pictures on the wall. Some showed him in his biking leathers and crash helmet at Goodwood racetrack in Sussex, where he loved to compete.

He'd always made such a success of everything. As well as his job as a salesman, he loved go-karting and his trophies took pride of place on his shelves.

As I looked at them, my gaze would always wander to that special container alongside them – the one holding Mark's ashes. We'd never discussed death with him, so we had no idea where he'd want his final resting place to be.

Everything else in my life had lost meaning. My marriage had begun to suffer and I'd contemplated suicide. Then, in May 1996, a concerned friend suggested I should visit a clairvoyant she'd been recommended.

Diana telephoned Jane:

My fingers trembled as I picked up the receiver. But before I could utter a word, a woman's voice said, 'You're ringing about your son Mark. He wants to talk to you.'

My head began to spin. How did she know his name? I was stunned. 'He's standing beside me holding a red rose in his hand,' continued Jane, 'the one you put in the coffin. When you come to see me, I'll tell you what he wants to say.' So, on 19 April 1996, 20 months after Mark's accident, I found myself going to see a perfect stranger about my son.

Jane started talking about Mark the moment I sat down in her living room. 'He's here in the room with us now, Diana,' she said. 'He's tall and good-looking. He's wearing jeans, a shirt and a blazer. He says the notes you put next to him in his coffin are still in his pocket.'

A strange feeling swept over me. I must have looked dazed. She couldn't possibly have known the things she told me. I looked around expecting to see Mark. Jane smiled. 'Only I can see him,' she explained gently. I imagined him standing close, his big beautiful brown eyes sparkling.

Jane also gave me other amazing facts about Mark that completely convinced me that he was not only with us but happy. He said how the accident was not his fault, how I still kept his Arai racing helmet and he talked of my feelings when I first saw his body. He joked about how after his death I'd had a photo of him enlarged. 'The bigger the better. I deserve it,' were his words. He spoke of how his friend Lee was still visiting car-boot sales and extended his thoughts for his motorcycle friends, especially David. He even said how I'd tried on his clothes – a fact that not even my husband knew – and how I had recently bought a large toy dog and laid it across his bed!

With tears streaming down my face I listened as she continued, 'Mark's worried about you. He says he wants you to get over his death. He's happy now and wants you to get on with your life. He says you should stop keeping his room as a shrine and that you must not hang on to his things any longer. He wants you to give them away. He's saying it's time to let go. One other thing: Mark says it's time to get rid of his ashes. He'd liked them to be scattered at Goodwood.'

I sat stunned. There was no doubt in my mind that the words were coming from Mark. 'But how can this be?' I stammered. 'He says to tell you it's like in the film *Ghost*,' she replied. 'He can see and hear everything that's going on.' Then she added, 'He's being called back to the spirit world now, Diana. He says he won't say goodbye, just that he'll see you later.'

When I returned home, I listened to the tape I'd made of Jane speaking. For the first time since Mark's death I felt a spark of hope. The following week, we went to Goodwood, as Mark had requested. 'Take care, my love,' I whispered as I sprinkled his ashes next to the starting line on the evening of Thursday, 2 May 1996.

Although it was difficult letting him go, as we drove back to our home in Southampton I felt as if a huge weight had lifted. 'This is a new beginning,' I thought to myself. 'It's what Mark wants.'

Over the following months, I began to sort through his belongings. It was difficult to part with them as I felt they were my last link with my son. But I've done it – the only thing I've kept is a tiny model of a motorbike Mark made just before he died. I no longer have to take medication for my depression and don't have to visit a counsellor. I know that without the help I have received from Mark and the Spirit World through Jane I certainly would have never recovered. Even worse, I would probably have committed the ultimate sin and taken my own life!

I owe Jane so much because she changed my life. I am now at peace with myself. I still see her sometimes and she always lets me know how Mark's getting on.

I still go to his room whenever I want to be with him. Knowing Mark's still with me is such a great comfort and, one day, I truly believe we'll meet up again.

Case File 3

Many of the things Jane and I have told our sitters have not been known to them at the time of their consultation, but have later been proved correct when they have checked the information with family and friends afterwards. This is important because it goes to prove that what we do is not mind-reading. This case file is about the special bond between mother and son, but in this case it is the mother who talks to her son from beyond.

Abandoned in a Moses basket on the steps of Dr Barnardo's home in London, Dudley Godfrey spent a lifetime wondering what his mother was like and why she would abandon him as a new-born baby:

> For years it was impossible to know the truth. I was not eligible for a birth certificate and Barnardo's refused to give me any informa-tion about my background. All I had was my fantasy. Perhaps my mother was unfit, a prostitute, or she just didn't want to know me. It's hard for anyone from a secure family to understand the inner anguish caused from not knowing who you are or what your roots are.

In 1995, when Dudley was 53, a charity worker called at his property business in Southampton. She was collecting for Dr Barnardo's. The lady informed him it was now easy for ex-Barnardo's children to obtain their birth certificate, and she explained to him how to go about getting his. A manager of a successful company, Dudley wasted no time in putting plans into action.

> I went straight down to the registrar and got the certificate. To my surprise I was born miles away. Next, I instructed my secretary to find out the name of the town's local parson and see if he knew anything about my family. Fortunately he was a keen genealogist and offered to check the parish records and write me a full family tree.
>
> When his report landed on my desk I dashed to the car and drove to London to see my last remaining relative – my mother's sister. Within an hour and a half I was at her doorstep, my heart pounding hard.

Dudley Godfrey discovered that his now dead father was the husband of his long-lost aunt. Clearly a terrible family problem had occurred at Dudley's birth that had resulted in his abandonment. At last Dudley knew who he was and a little about his background.

> The most startling thing was meeting my half-brother. He was my clone. Not only did he look like me but he had the same body language and even talked like me. Sadly I also discovered that my mother had died a long time ago, and I resigned myself to the fact there was no way I would ever talk to her or know her.

Soon afterwards Dudley read an article about my work. The article described how I could talk with people who have gone over into the spirit world. Dudley telephoned me and arranged an appointment.

> Immediately I walked into his consultation room Craig asked me if I knew of an Uncle George, who he said had been talking to him during his meditations. George, who I had called Uncle, had brought me up after I left Barnardo's at the age of two. 'He died of TB,' said Craig, 'and says that his wife's name was Lotty. Also, he would have been very sceptical about mediums as he'd had a very strict religious upbringing. He loved the countryside and was a farm labourer.'
>
> I couldn't believe what I was hearing. Craig was reeling off the facts. Facts that he could never have checked through public records. By now tears were rolling down my cheeks.
>
> Craig continued by saying, 'There's something about him that only you and he ever knew about. George tells me that he was a secret

drinker.' That clinched it. I was the only person in the world that knew this. It was a standing joke between us.'

Craig went on to tell me about how I'd been in Dr Barnardo's. He told me about my deceased wife Betty and that she was aware that I'd been having problems with my kidneys and how she wanted to pass on her love to my daughter and two sons. She was pleased, Craig said, that despite everything I was making a success of my life and was reasonably happy.

Then perhaps the most important person of all came through. 'I've got to give you a message from a lady with the name Grace,' I said to Dudley. 'She died of womb cancer at the age of 30 and she's so sorry for everything that happened when you were little.

At last Dudley's mother had made contact. 'Your mum is telling me that she didn't want to give you to Dr Barnardo's. It broke her heart but there was nothing that she could do. She was forced to do what she did, there was no way she could keep you, and she regretted it for the rest of her short life. She loves you, her only child, very much.' Dudley takes up the story:

Craig told me that I must ask my aunt about this and various other events that transpired at the time of my birth. Immediately afterwards I telephoned my aunt and asked her about all the things that were said during the consultation. She was dumbfounded. 'How on earth do you know these things!' she exclaimed. But that was Mum's and my little secret.

I am not in the habit of visiting psychics or mediums. For me, it was my first and perhaps only exposure to these things. But it helped me a great deal and unloaded a tremendous weight from my shoulders. At last I believe that I have been able to talk to the mother that I never knew. I now have a photograph of Mum, but the greatest comfort of all is knowing that her spirit is close to me and that one day we will meet and talk about everything that happened. My life-long fear that I would never be able to talk to her just isn't true.

Fortune-telling

Although mediumship is primarily about proving that we survive death and bringing comfort and solace to the bereaved, there are times when the spirit world makes contact in order to give a warning about the future. Unfortunately most people have no idea of how superior mediumship is to fortune-telling. Some insist I just read the Tarot cards as they want 'nothing to do with spooks and all that'.

I have spoken to my Tibetan spirit guide about this. The Spiritualist part of me believes in free will and that we should take 'personal responsibility' for our destiny. The Tibetan Buddhist influences around me tell of the principles of karma and acceptance. In addition I believe in reincarnation and that I am influenced by two of my past lives as a somewhat rebellious Tibetan monk. (I believe one of these lives may have been around about 1230 when Genghis Khan and the Mongols dominated the world scene, and another at about 1650 as a painter of mandalas during the time of the fifth Dalai Lama.)

My main concern about fortune-telling is that people will become either spiritually paralysed if they are told something bad about the future, or complacent if they are shown something good. Most people see a fortune-teller because they are unable to cope with their worry. They just want someone to tell them that everything will be all right.

In answer to my questions my Tibetan spirit guide told me that the objective of divination is to assess the person's situation and recommend ways to respond to it and take remedial action. Although there is no escaping their karma they can trigger the latent positive potential in themselves and others. In this way the individual is not stepping outside of the laws of cause and effect but instead using merit to awaken the forces of good karma.

Another spiritual influence in my life supersedes even this advice: our living 'guru' Sathya Sai Baba (see Chapter Ten). I apply his simple advice to my spiritual and predictive work, which I believe says it all: 'Speak soft and sweet; sympathise with suffering and loss and ignorance; try your best to apply the salve of soothing words and timely succour.'

Case File 4

When Joan B. came to see me, the spirit world was quick to give her advice about the future. Apparently she had booked the consultation with me to see if I could give her any insight into the sorry state of her marriage. I told her, 'If you don't act immediately, I see you losing everything.' Joan goes on:

> Craig communicated with many people I'd known who had passed into the spirit. In particular he spoke to my Nan who told him that her

wedding ring had broken in two. This had happened recently and Craig said it was also a symbol of what was happening in my own life.

'Your husband owns a restaurant,' said Craig. 'You must be very, very careful as he's trying to sell it without you finding out.' Craig was right, we did own a restaurant but it would be impossible for him to sell it. It had only been open for two years and who would buy a restaurant that had traded for such a short time?

Craig insisted that I make enquiries. If I didn't act, he said, the money would disappear to America and I'd be left with nothing. He said that a female solicitor would help me get a court order to prohibit the sale. The judge would look favourably upon my case.

It was Joan's grandparents who were telling me all this information from the spirit world. Her grandmother told me many facts about herself, but one fact in particular proved to Joan that it was her:

Craig said that my grandmother had two wedding rings and that I now had one and my sister the other, which was right. He also identified the problems that I was having with my daughter and how to deal with them.

Immediately after the consultation Joan employed a female solicitor and asked her to make enquiries about the restaurant. She discovered that it was for sale and a buyer had been found. Joan also heard rumours that her husband was planning to move to America:

We went to court immediately we knew the facts and took out an injunction to stop the sale. The result was that I and my two children were given a fair settlement and received a substantial sum of money. If I hadn't listened to the clairvoyant we would now be destitute. I've still got a lot of emotional problems to resolve but at least now our financial future is secure.

Case File 5

People come to see Jane and myself for all sorts of reasons. Tracey Roberts needed advice about a neighbour who was causing trouble. She found out much more than she bargained for. Tracey explains:

'You're either a hairdresser or something to do with television,' was the first thing Craig said when I sat down for the psychic consultation. He could never have guessed that I'd just embarked on a career as an actress. 'Although you've come along today to sort out a material problem there's something more important you should know about. Although you are black, your step-father Jim was white. He wants you to know that you've a four-year-old sister who you've never met, but who one day will want to get in touch with you.

I had a sneaking feeling that what Craig was saying was true, but had never really wanted to face up to it. There were family rumours, but I'd always thought that they were just that – rumours.

Tracey was also given the information she needed about her neighbour dispute. I told her how it was a Chinese lady with a disabled child who was causing the problem, but there was some good news from the spirit world – the lady would be moving soon and everybody, including the Chinese lady and her son, would be happy. I also told Tracey about her friend Ronnie, who had died of bowel cancer.

I had no idea how she had died but found out later it was bowel cancer – just as Craig had said. When I got home I decided to check out what Craig had said about my lost half-sister. I hadn't seen my father since I was ten years old and it wasn't the sort of question I wanted to ask Mum. My only option was to ask my sister in Jamaica. At first she wasn't forthcoming when I rang her, but when she discovered how much I already knew the true facts came out. Yes, we did have a half-sister – and she had just had her fourth birthday.

Most people, at some time in their life, have had a psychic experience. The readers' letters I publish in my newspaper columns represent only a fraction of the thousands sent to me. It appears that many people – perhaps everyone – have the potential to be psychic. However, not everyone should take it up professionally. To know what your clients are going through you have to have suffered yourself. You need to know what it is to have the most important things in your life taken away from you.

Case File 6

Unlike many of the cases we have looked at so far, Bob Morris is no stranger to psychic phenomena. He is himself a Spiritualist healer and regularly visits mediums to keep in touch with those he knows in the afterlife. He says:

I can't understand why so many people are antagonistic to the claims of mediums and healers. I have been involved in the subject for a great many years and have been guided and helped by the spirit people throughout my life. I believe that mediumship can really help people overcome grief and offers a wonderful philosophy for life.

When Bob came for a consultation with me, as the sitting progressed I said, 'You're a very lucky man. Fortune has smiled upon you just recently. You've had a windfall and you should expect another soon.' Unbeknown to me, Bob had, only a few weeks before, won a Jackpot £50,000 on a scratch card for the National Lottery. He explains:

> Strangely enough I woke up that morning and just knew that I was going to win. I remembered the time from long ago when I had the same feeling. On that occasion we were very hard up and the last thing the family could afford was a Sunday joint – it cost over two shillings! I announced that I'd win on the Tuesday and said so every day. Nobody believed me by the time Saturday arrived. By 2 o'clock I had a big leg of pork in my hands. I'd won first prize in the raffle!
>
> As before, I announced to the world that I would be winning the National Lottery that week. Already I had been quite lucky and had won four out of five first prizes at our church's raffle. A few days later I hit the Jackpot.
>
> Craig told me all about this story during the consultation and there's no way he could have known I'd won. But he told me that I'd win again. And I'm sure he's right.

We'll keep you posted.

The afterlife

Most people fear death, and when we lose someone we love, the greatest insult to their memory is to refrain from talking about them for fear of upsetting the bereaved. But when a medium makes contact with the afterworld it is rarely a sombre occasion. There are no darkened rooms, no spooky castles or creaking walls. The 'dead' like to prove to those of us left behind that they are happy in their new life, and they sometimes pull our leg and joke with us. When a spirit enters the otherworld they are shown the mistakes and errors of their life on earth but their basic personality does not change very much. Often the objective of their communication is just to let us know that the suffering of their passing illness is gone and that they are still the same person we know and love.

One of the main reasons people say they go to see a medium is just to know that the one they love is all right. They may remember the terrible ordeal that their loved one went through on their deathbed, or have seen the personality changes that drugs and brain illness brings. After such terrible things could they possibly be made whole again when they enter the afterlife?

It is wonderful to know the truth that once the spirit is free of the physical body, a feeling of health and harmony returns almost instantly. However, some spirits may need a little help after passing over and are taken to a place known by Spiritualists as the 'Halls of Healing'. Here the trauma of transition and the residue of illness from earthly life is finally dissolved. Life-long illnesses may take the spirit doctors a little while to cure, but cure them they do. In time, the spirit person is brought back to the natural harmony and health that is their essential nature. The paranoid schizophrenic finds peace, all bodily ailments disappear and the crippled walk – even fly.

Case File 7

Rosemary Stokes nursed her desperately ill husband Ray for 18 months at home. In time, as his condition and pain became intolerable, there was no choice but to take him to a hospice. Ray had cancer. He was terminally ill. Rosemary goes on:

> It was a terrible ordeal. He was in a lot of pain and very frightened. We loved each other so much and I used to sit by his bedside, wiping the tears from his eyes. To see that dreadful pallor in my love's face was awful. He had been such a handsome and dignified man but slowly everything was being taken away from him. We were living a nightmare, yet when he finally passed away on the 31 January it was a terrible shock even though I'd had plenty of time to prepare myself.

In March, Rosemary heard about my work as a medium, and wondered whether I would be able to communicate with her beloved Ray:

> I'd never had proof, but in my heart I believed that there's an afterlife. All I wanted to know was that Ray was all right.

Craig told me that Ray was showing him a gold signet ring with a black stone. It was broken and I should get it mended and wear it. Absolutely nobody knew this. Craig told me about Ray's sense of humour and that he said, 'Didn't I really look the part all dressed in blue!' We'd buried Ray in a blue suit. He mentioned how he'd met up with his friend Joey who'd died only two years before, how he hadn't been insured and how we'd planted a rose tree in his memory. Together they were raising their glasses of Bacardi to me – it was the only alcohol Ray would ever drink. And astonishingly Craig went on to say that Ray was telling him that when he was in the coffin my daughter had pinned a gold heart onto his lapel.

To me it was like winning the lottery. Craig described all the terrible suffering that Ray went through, but that like Ray I should put this memory in the past. I needed to let go of those dreadful memories of his illness and know that my Ray was no longer in pain. Although he'd been frightened when he died, Ray said that the fear vanished as soon as he saw his father come for him to take him into the better world in which he lived now. I came away from the consultation feeling a lot, lot better.

Case File 8

It is reassuring to know that the one you love is safe in their new world, but some spirit communicators are more than all right, they are ecstatic in loving their new found world. When Jan Hartnet visited me, the last thing she expected was to be splitting her sides with laughter:

Craig opened by asking if I knew a man who had passed over called Charlie, who came from Limerick in Ireland. Of course I did – he was my much-loved uncle. Craig added, however, that, although everyone called him Charlie, the name on his birth certificate was Joseph, which was absolutely right.

Craig then said that Charlie was telling him that he'd died of a chest complaint during the month of September, but that Charlie was such a joker that it was going to be hard to keep a straight face.

Charlie also said, now that he was dead, his wife would have nobody to nag at – she should have had him stuffed – which was exactly Charlie's type of humour. He said that I was deluding myself sitting there, because there was no afterlife! 'There's nothing here at all – don't bother coming,' he joked.

By this time we were falling about with laughter as Uncle Charlie fired joke after joke at Craig. But this was exactly as Charlie was. He couldn't open his mouth without saying something funny.

Craig stopped the consultation for five minutes so that we could compose ourselves, and then continued. He asked Charlie to give some proof that it really was him. 'He tells me that your brother is a fire-man,' said Craig. 'Your dad was a bingo caller and has also just had a major operation but is okay now. He says that you've a daughter called Laurie and she has four interests in life: boys, music, boys and music.' We started to chuckle again at the last comment. But Craig was absolutely right.

Craig also said that Charlie was joking about my car's exhaust pipe – on the day I visited Charlie in hospital before he died, the exhaust fell off my car. It was another thing he'd pulled my leg about.

'You shouldn't drink so much,' said Craig. 'Charlie says that you should stick to tea like he did.' Charlie was a constant tea-drinker. Craig started laughing again. 'Oh my God! He's just said "Mother's going to lose her purse yet again!" My mother had lost her purse only days before and, shortly after the reading, she lost it again. Craig went on, 'You should know this. Last week you bought yourself a set of Tarot cards – but you don't have a clue how to use them!'

During the consultation Jan also spoke to her sister who told her that she was looking after the stillborn baby she'd lost, and that she'd been trying to let her know this by surrounding her with the song of children:

Strangely enough, every morning when I woke up I'd hear children's voices but could never fathom where they'd been coming from.

Charlie's message to Jan was that, no matter how gloomy life looks, there's always a bright side:

Laughter was just the tonic I needed at that time. Sometimes I now dream of Charlie on his bike and wake up feeling cheerful. Charlie told me that life for me was going to get much better – and it has.

Case File 9

Schoolteacher Pam Dibble loves kids. When Pam's 11-year-old daughter Charlotte died from an asthma attack she was devastated. Charlotte had already tried to contact her mum from the other side:

After she died the light in her room would flicker and on one occasion her cassette recorder started playing by itself. It was a recording Charlotte had made of her playing the keyboards. I checked the machine and there were no batteries in it!

When we moved house I went into Charlotte's old bedroom just to say 'goodbye'. I turned the light on and the bulb exploded with a loud bang, leaving just a bare, burnt, dangling, wire. Call it coincidence if you like – but for me that was Charlotte saying a last goodbye.

It was Pam's mother who made the first link from the other side when we began the sitting at her home. She had already been around Pam and clearly had been preparing the lines of communication. Pam goes on:

One of the first things that Craig said to me was, 'I've your mother here showing herself standing by a wardrobe. And, it may seem odd but she's holding a new set of towels.' This immediately made sense. Only a few days before, I was surprised to find, in the wardrobe, a brand new set of towels that had been hers.

Craig told me lots of correct things about Mum such as her having water retention in her legs and getting fat even though she couldn't eat towards the end. Craig said that Mum wanted to remind me of a funny story that no medium could research in records. Craig told me that she was laughing as she told of how she had lost her false teeth while leaning out of a train window. This had been a long-standing family joke – she had lost them, as Craig had said, and remained toothless for two years. She was buried without dentures.

It was Charlotte whom I really desperately wanted to contact. Craig said that he saw her by me holding a teddy bear. 'There's something odd about the teddy,' said Craig. 'It was buried with her... but there's something missing'. Charlotte was indeed buried with her teddy. It had a missing ear.

What convinced me it was Charlotte was when Craig said that she was now singing 'The Owl and the Pussycat Went to Sea'. Just before she died Charlotte had done a beautiful illustration of the Edward Lear poem. It had won first prize in the school competition. On the same day that she was being buried her sister collected the school prize on Charlotte's behalf.

One of the reasons that this sitting was so precise was because Pam's mum was able to break the ice by making her laugh by reminding her of the funny story about the false teeth. The story was no doubt encouraged by my spirit helpers who work with me and organize the people communicating on the other side. If there's a funny story about false teeth, my spirit helper will make sure that it's communicated. I think he finds it fun and it certainly does help to lighten the atmosphere.

I remember telling one lady that her 'dead' father was laughing about how she had put his false teeth in her handbag and had taken them with her to his funeral. She told me afterwards that there was a panic on the day and she had rushed to the undertakers with his false teeth so that he could be buried with dignity. She was too late and put them in her handbag and secretly carried them with her throughout the solemn proceedings.

Case File 10

Reuniting dead children with their parents has also been an important part of Jane's mediumistic work. She has helped countless mothers to reunite with their dead children and many a tear of mixed sorrow and joy has been shed. When Pauline Bennett's only son had a fatal heart attack only yards from her home it seemed to her that everything was lost, but Robert soon let his mum know he was all right. 'I saw him in his bedroom. He just stood there smiling at me. People said it was just my mind playing tricks but I saw him as real as you or I.' Pauline's belief that her son continued in a new life was confirmed when she and her husband had a reading with Jane:

> The first person to speak to me from the spirit world was a friend of the family who, Jane correctly said, was a German nurse. She was helping Robert from the other side. When Jane spoke to Robert she gave excellent proof: his name, date of passing and the like. And Jane said how pleased he was that we had bought a memorial garden seat in his honour.
>
> She also described how Robert had been buried wearing his yellow football shirt and even gave its number. About three-quarters of the way through the reading there was a voice in the room that we all heard clearly. 'Mum,' it cried out. We were all dumbstruck to hear Robert's voice.
>
> Jane said that Robert was concerned about our friend Natasha who was about to undergo open-heart surgery. Jane said she would concentrate every night and send her some absent healing. The doctors really couldn't believe what they were seeing. Natasha recovered from her operation in record time.

Case File 11

When I first started working as a medium it used to worry me a great deal if some of the information I was saying was wrong. Sometimes your own thoughts do get muddled with those that are being projected from the spirit world, but more often than not it is information that the sitter doesn't know about which they have to verify later. Jane and I believe that it is the evidence which needs to confirmed by a third party that is the most important, as it proves to us that what we're doing is not mind-reading. This can be seen in the case of Jackie Lucas:

> When Craig said that he was in touch with a man named Frank who died in his sleep I realized that he was talking about Dad. What convinced me was when he explained that he had been reading a war novel by Wilbur Smith just before he died – which was exactly right. Craig said that he was now feeling happy over in the other world and that he had met up with my step-father Ernest who had died in terribly tragic circumstances. He described events that even the closest of our family don't know.
>
> But there were things that Craig said that just didn't make sense. He kept saying that Frank and Ernest shared a love of cricket and that they would talk about it at the pub all the time. Craig said that Dad had even lived near a cricket ground. This was news to me, but I did know someone who had lived near a cricket ground. 'I'm not referring to George,' piped up Craig. 'He lived in a flat overlooking the Oval in London – I'm talking about Dad's interest.' Craig was right about George, but I was sure that he was wrong about Dad and Ernest.

Jackie decided to check out the details with her Mum. Jackie's Mum had very much wanted to attend the sitting, but had backed out at the last minute – the tragedy of her husband's death was still too painful to think about.

> Mum confirmed that years ago, when they owned a pub, Dad and Ernest talked incessantly about cricket and their house at the time overlooked the school cricket grounds in Winchester.
>
> Craig had also said that there was a funny family story about Dad losing money over some chickens. Well, he got that right too. One year Dad had decided to buy a load of chickens to fatten up and sell

at Christmas for a profit. But when it came to the time to kill them Dad just couldn't do it. He had to pay someone the profits to do it for him.

Jackie's Mum shed a few tears when she told her the things that her Dad had said to prove that he was all right in his new life.

I nearly didn't go to see Craig. I was afraid that I'd burst into tears at the mere mention of Dad. But it helped Mum and me tremendously. Just to know that Dad's his same humorous self is enough. I'm glad I went.

Case File 12

Jane's mediumistic evidence of survival can be just as accurate, as in the following case of Debbie Stuart and her three-year-old son Mike. One night Mike came to his Mum saying, 'Mummy, I've just seen Jamie in my bedroom.' The psychic child's night visions were of 32-year-old James Percy who had died a few months before. 'He would have long conversations with my dead friend,' says Debbie. 'There were things mentioned in his cheerful, one-way conversation that Mike could never have known about.' The first time that Debbie went for a sitting with Jane, Jamie Percy made himself known:

I was only expecting fortune-telling, but Jane said that a man named Jamie was trying to communicate through her. He wanted to reassure his mother that he was all right. 'He died of a massive heart attack at work,' Jane said, 'and he's showing me the docks and is carrying bags of cement... no, it's not cement; it's bags of flour!'

Jamie had died two weeks before Christmas from a massive heart coronary outside the Rank Flour Mills at Southampton Docks. He was unloading flour from his lorry. Debbie passed the message on to Jamie's mother, Joyce. Joyce also attended a sitting with Jane. She goes on:

The first thing that Jane said to me was that she saw him with a bunch of red roses. 'Is there a wedding anniversary soon?' asked Jane. In fact it was Arthur's and my anniversary the next day.

Jane continued with the subject of flowers. She then said that my mother was with her also and she brought freesias – they were her favourite flowers. Also she said, 'Jamie is talking about crocus bulbs.

You're not to plant any more on his grave. There's far too many of them now.' When I had gone on my regular visit to his grave a week before I had been surprised how many crocuses there were on the grave. It was absolutely covered in them. In fact we had planted one lot too deep and subsequently planted a second lot. Both came up this year and now, as Jane had said, the grave was overrun.

Jane went on, 'I see a man like the racing driver Graham Hill... is there something about racing cars... no, not racing cars, banger cars?'

Joyce explained that her son had been a well-known banger racer. She showed me, after the interview, a video tribute that Matchams Park Racing had made for her. It included Jamie's races and the two minutes' silence that the stadium had requested from the normally noisy crowd. There was complete silence; James Percy was clearly a much loved and respected young man – over 300 people had attended his funeral. Joyce continues:

Jane said so many other things to me that proved beyond doubt that she was indeed communicating with Jamie. She saw the pair of shoes of his that I still kept, our oval locket containing his hair that was cut just before the burial, his love of music (she said correctly that they played 'There is a green hill far away' at the funeral) and talked about Jamie's son Sam (from a previous relationship) whom we had unwillingly lost touch with. Jane also described Jamie's friend Sid, who she said regularly visited the grave together with his little dog and how he used to have to buy endless curries for his girlfriend at the time. She said that he was holding a cake shaped like a kitchen sink that I'd made and that at Easter I'd be making another very unusual cake. She could hear the song 'Twinkle, twinkle, little star'.

For a joke Jamie had asked me to make a kitchen sink cake for his girlfriend as she was constantly complaining that she was forever standing at the kitchen sink. And Jane's prediction about the new cake came to pass. I am a helper at the local play group – another fact that Jane picked up – and for the Easter draw they asked me if I would make a cake in the shape of a giant yellow Easter egg. The school children were singing 'Twinkle, twinkle, little star' when they asked me!

Jamie's father, Arthur, who has been a down-to-earth dairy farmer for forty-two years, admits that he was at first very sceptical when his wife told him about the sitting with Jane:

On the evening after Joyce spoke to Jane I clearly saw a figure in our room. There was a cold chill and it walked through the door. I took it to be Jamie. In the morning we received a telephone call from Debbie. 'Little Mike says that Jamie won't be visiting our house anymore,' said Debbie. 'He's gone over to visit you instead.'

Sometimes people are surprised by my bad memory. When they talk to me after a public demonstration of mediumship they realize that I have forgotten all the things I said only moments ago. The reason, I believe, is that if we mediums were to retain all the memories of death, illness, and heartache that the spirit world show us, then it could cause us severe psychological anxieties. Instead, we are a channel for communication. The impressions come and go. They are washed from our thoughts as soon as they are spoken.

Chapter Six
Evil Spirits

Many people enjoy the thrill of a good horror film, but it is less entertaining when strange and frightening things start happening in reality. Hollywood film-makers did not invent the phenomena of ghosts, spectres and poltergeists – they just exaggerate the truth and throw in extra special effects. 'Earthbound' spirits, as they are called in medium circles, can cause havoc to the people of this world. Although nobody, in the case files that follow, spits green slime, crawls out of graves or levitates, for the people concerned what happened was much more frightening because they didn't watch the events on the big screen, but experienced them in reality.

Case File 1

Lis Glen's stepson, Lee, was 17 when in 1988, for a dare, he and four friends decided to experiment with a ouija board. 'Four of you will die,' it spelled out. Lis recalls:

> When Lee told his dad, Ken, and me that he was going to die, we thought he was joking. We had no idea that he and his four friends had been messing with an ouija board.

About a week later Lee was dead. He was attacked on New Year's Eve and, during the fight, his head was banged against the pavement several times. Since then two others who used the board have died in tragic circumstances. Lis continues:

> Lee collapsed a few days after the fight while baby-sitting for my other son's children. He was rushed into hospital and put on a life-support machine. We were told he was suffering a delayed reaction to the bangs to his head and that he'd be severely brain-damaged if he came out of his coma. But on the tenth day, pneumonia set in and he just slipped away.

A few months later, one of the other boys caught pneumonia while camping and died. It was a shock as he'd been so healthy.

That's when one of Lee's other friends came to see us. He was in total panic and told us about the ouija board. It all seemed so ridiculous to us. But this year, another of the group took his own life, leaving only two out of the five.

Lee's passing was a terrible blow to the whole Glen family. Not only did they suffer the shock of his death, but there was also an inquest to follow. His father found the pressure too much to bear; there were arguments in the family and he gradually sank into a deep depression. Lee must have seen all this from the spirit world. He tried to make contact, as Lis explains:

A few weeks after Lee died, strange things had begun to happen to us. One time, Ken and I were watching television when we heard footsteps upstairs. We thought we were being burgled – but when we checked, the room was empty. It really scared us.

And that was just the beginning. Another night, I put the kettle on and then left the kitchen. When I came back, it was unplugged and on the other side of the sink from where it normally is – and it was cold, despite having been boiled once already. Then a picture that had been hanging in the hall for years fell off the wall for no apparent reason. We also started to lose things and, despite turning the house upside down, we never did find them. Even when we moved house this year strange things happened. Ken was making an aviary and a pot full of screws and nails completely disappeared.

We began to wonder if it was Lee's way of trying to keep in touch, and decided to look for help. It was then we heard of the mediums Craig and Jane Hamilton-Parker.

Lis and Ken came to see Jane and myself at a mystics' fair. Lis had a reading with me and, at the same time, Ken went to Jane's table close by. Lis had overcome her grief, but Ken was still suffering from severe depression – he told me later that it had become so bad that he was even seeing a psychologist for help. The psychologist apparently said later that Ken seeing us had been therapeutic.

Lee seemed to communicate with us both simultaneously:

Jane did a reading for Ken and attempted to tap into Lee. She said things that only Lee and Ken could possibly know – that Lee's motorbike had been traded in for a CD-player, and that when he died his hair was a funny colour – he'd dyed it just before he collapsed.

Jane and Craig have told us the strange occurrences are Lee's way of saying he's okay. Until we met Jane and Craig we'd known nothing but sorrow – now I hope we've reached the turning point.

Was the death of Lee Glen really predicted by the ouija board, or was his and the two subsequent passings more a case of coincidence and self-fulfilled prophecy? Methods of spirit contact like ouija boards are subject to all sorts of influences that may not be spirit people at all. Jane and I are inclined to believe that the 'occurrences' around the house may be Lee's way of trying to communicate, but perhaps other mental powers influenced the board. As Jane says, 'This is an exceptional case, but I don't honestly think the attack on Lee can be connected to the teenagers sitting around the ouija board.'

The Spiritualist Newspaper, *Psychic News*, asked Eileen Roberts, president of the Institute of Spiritualist Mediums and lecturer on mediumistic development, about the case and how easily the subconscious mind can govern ouija board messages. She responded:

This could have been a genuine communication warning the teenagers, but we are generally ignorant of the many things the mind can do. It is easy for susceptible people, especially teenagers, to be emotionally upset by such a message.

Although she admitted that the attack on Lee was unlikely to be any kind of self-fulfilled prophecy, she speculated there may have been elements of this in the other two deaths:

All you need is for one person to believe such a prediction and it sparks off others. Perhaps the boy who caught pneumonia on the camping trip decided he was going to die anyway and felt less inclined to resist it. For a trained medium the ouija board can be a legitimate method of spirit communication, but the general ignorance about how they work is such that I often feel like gathering them all together and burning the lot.

There is an interesting postscript to this case file. About a year after Lis Glen had her consultations with us, a young lady called Jackie S. came for a sitting with me. Immediately I had to tell her about her brother, a young man with the name Richard, who died on St Valentine's Day from pneumonia. I described how he was a bit of a rebel, had a sarcastic sense of humour, could be lazy and smoked roll-up tobacco. He joked about himself and I felt him urging me to reassure his sister that he was all right and hadn't changed much since he passed over to the spirit side.

'My death was predicted,' I heard Richard say. 'I was one of the lads who played with the ouija board with Lee. Tell Alan that he'll be okay. He'll have a long and happy life.' I repeated what I was told to Jackie, who by now was in tears. When we had begun the sitting I had no idea that she was connected through the tragedy with Lis Glen's family.

The next day I contacted Lis Glen's son Alan. When I mentioned the ouija board incident he visibly shuddered. But when I went on to give him Richard's message it was as if the burden of years of worry was lifted from his shoulders. Alan now runs a successful printing business. He's happily married and I'm sure that one day he will be a very prosperous man.

Case File 2

In the right hands the spirit communication methods of ouija boards, planchettes and table-tilting are quite safe. But it is very important to make sure that the work is done in an atmosphere of love and sincerity. If this vital ingredient is missing, then chaos results, as the following story from Di Spottiswood illustrates:

> For twenty years I have kept quiet about the frightening things I saw. But now I feel I must speak out in order to warn others of the dangers of playing with ouija boards.
>
> It all started as a game, when some teenage friends of mine started using the ouija board. An old man who once owned the country bungalow in which the seance was being held started to communicate through the board. Other neighbours became interested in what was going on and soon quite a crowd would visit to watch the proceedings.
>
> But the language used became abusive and foul – which amused the 'players' who answered back with similar tones. I was called in to help when things started to go very badly wrong.
>
> Everybody blamed everybody else when swear words started to appear on the walls. But there was no arguing when articles started whizzing through the air and narrowly missing the small children.

Incredibly, wardrobes moved around as though they were made of matchwood, voices were heard, bumps and bangs sounded all through the night – and the whole family became absolutely terrified. I saw burly, muscular men tremble with terror on seeing these things.

The worse thing I saw myself was the unshaven face of an old man push through the kitchen wall. I saw it happen. It was as plain as day. And as it happened I felt a burning sensation from head to toe.

I spent hours on the phone trying to track down someone who could help us. Finally I managed to find a medium brave enough to go along. She identified a young 17-year-old girl as the source of the energy that fuelled the poltergeist activity. The medium's involvement helped, but the bungalow never completely returned to normal. The family eventually had to move.

It has often been known for poltergeist activity to be centred around teenagers in puberty, and the medium may have been right in identifying the 17-year-old girl as the source of the activity. However, it is more likely that the crowd of participants fuelled the poltergeist with negative psychic energy. For centuries the Tibetan yogis studied this and called these entities *Tulpas*. They can cause havoc for a short period but inevitably, given time, their energy dissipates and the activity ceases.

Case File 3

When John and Joyce Allen moved into their new house the last thing they expected was to be transported into a series of events worthy of a programme from the *X-Files*. John explains:

It all started ten years ago when items in our house started to go missing and were returned to another location. There was no logical reason to explain what kept happening. It wasn't caused by absent-mindedness, or children and pets carrying off the objects – there was no logical explanation.

Soon we discovered that my neighbours were all experiencing similar things. In particular, the house two doors along saw items flying around, electrical switches switching themselves back on, a piano playing by itself; a dog was also heard and items flew through the air and even around corners.

Most people assumed it was the ghost of a lady called Anny Moody and her dog, who used to own the old Canal Wharf House Inn. It was a house of ill repute at the turn of the century and was demolished in 1982. Many claim to have seen Anny's ghost walking our street.

I did some research and discovered that the houses were built directly on a ley line which is where 'earth energies' are said to accumulate. And the house where the poltergeist activity happened was built exactly on the intersection of two major ley lines. As far as I could discover, there had only been one death on our road since the 1950s.

The ghost of a small boy with callipers was also seen by myself and many people. He had died, he told us, during World War I and was looking for his father, who had been killed in France along with so many others in the Flanders fields. I was unable to trace the boys address in the records.

After three years of strange paranormal activity John and Joyce had had enough. Joyce goes on:

I called in our local Spiritualists to assist the trapped spirit people to move on into the other realms. I sat with them in the seance and I have to say it was a very strange experience indeed. I felt the pain and suffering of the various soldier's wounds as they communicated through the medium.

We concluded that the soldiers and a World War II pilot were trapped by the energy of the ley line and the crippled boy with his dog had been trying to attract our attention to help free his friends.

The Spiritualists now appear to have exorcised the ghosts, and buried various crystals around the area to disperse the ley line's energy. John did some further research and the soldier explanation appears logical. The houses on our road were once owned, I discovered, by the MoD.

Ley lines

Parapsychologists have found that many of the most famous poltergeist cases have happened at the intersection of two ley lines. These are said to be a network of earth energy lines that crisscross the country. The prehistoric inhabitants of ancient Britain were supposedly aware of these lines of force and built their monuments on the most important concentrations of these fields. Stonehenge is a prime example.

I am aware that these events caused the family severe distress which resulted in many problems. Persistent earthbound spirits can be very disruptive and it's often the Spiritualists that get called in to sort matters out.

It is unusual for Spiritualists to identify the source of a haunting as the node of intersecting ley lines, but times are changing. I believe that their diagnosis was right. The earth does have areas of negative energy where nasty elemental powers can accumulate. Many people now believe that these negative areas are places where 'earth rays' that rise up from the centre of the earth are distorted by underground streams and rock strata. A negative geopathic area will make a person feel uneasy, tired and tense. Because of this some places just don't feel right and can even cause illness in people who inhabit these places.

As well as centring on areas of geopathic stress, the energy required for poltergeist activity and vivid hauntings can accumulate because of water. In some cases underground streams and covered wells supply the energy. In the next case file, it may have been the sea itself.

Case File 4

A committee member of one of our local Spiritualist churches telephoned us one evening to explain that they had a problem:

> A lady has contacted the church and claims that she and her husband are being attacked by a poltergeist. Someone or something has been throwing objects around the cabin of their boat on the Solent and, she says, it has also been attacking her. We sent along one of our local mediums and he feels that this is a real phenomenon and not just a figment of an overworked imagination. He felt, however, that it would be best if a strong group of mediums could be assembled to tackle the problem together. He is convinced that it is real as there's a strong and violent presence on board. Would you two be prepared to help?

Jane and I agreed to go along, and a date was fixed for the following Saturday night. We were told that the occurrences happened mainly at night, so this would be the best time to have our seance. There would be five of us taking part – we'd have enough psychic power between us all to make a serious challenge to the poltergeist.

It was on the Friday night before that we realized that this was going to be a real case of a haunting. Something happened that shook us both. Jane and I were lying in bed, talking about our plans for the encounter the next night. We were both relaxed and feeling quiet, peaceful and at ease. Our conversation was interrupted when the room lit up with an intense blinding white light. We both sat bolt upright in bed. My immediate thought was that it was lightning but the weather forecast had already predicted that it would be a clear evening with no threat of thunderstorms or rain.

There was a second brilliant flash and the room remained illuminated for some time. The light then folded in on itself and formed into a luminous ball, about four foot across, in the centre of the room and floating at about head height.

Jane and I sat speechless as it hovered for what seemed like an eternity, but what in reality must have been about thirty seconds. It then shot across the room, out of the door, and toward the living room. I leaped out of bed and gave chase. Seconds later it disappeared leaving no trace.

Jane and I had seen things like this before but never with such an intensity. As a young child I would experience a ball of light that seemed to read my thoughts – a manifestation of spirit perhaps? Jane had also had a peculiar experience one day while alone with her then nine-year-old daughter Chantal from her first marriage:

> Chantal and I saw a ball of orange light about a foot across, hovering in the living room. It moved towards us and hovered in the air about three feet in front of us. Chantal was becoming frightened as I put my hand out and tried to touch it. My hand went straight through it. There was a swishing sound as the ball of light bounced onto the television and out of the window.'

However, Jane and I had never seen anything as brilliant as that Friday night's manifestation. We were both, to say the least, startled by the experience, but we didn't feel that we had encountered anything malicious. Indeed, the room felt peaceful with a sense of well-being.

It did affect us physically, though. We both felt sick, and there was a sickly scent in the air. We were sweating, and for both of us the solar plexus region (just below the rib cage) felt uncomfortable – as if it was knotted. I have read of similar reactions in physical circles, where the mediums manifest ectoplasm, although Jane and I do not claim to be physical mediums.

Surprisingly, the whole experience startled but didn't frighten us. We believed that a spirit from the higher realms had visited us to reassure us that we were well protected and to prepare us for the next night. The angels were looking after us.

It was already beginning to get dark when we met the other mediums who would be going on board the old converted fishing boat, which looked ominous and creepy against the darkening sky. It creaked and groaned as it rocked with the tide. The sultry evening was turning colder and across the river we could see the lights of other boats bobbing up and down. The moon was casting its first rays on the indigo waters.

We kept the mood light by joking between ourselves. With this type of situation it's best not to be too sombre or serious. Jane and I had spent some time before in deep meditation to prepare ourselves, and had by now opened our psychic awareness. The lady who was having the problem was clearly troubled. Her aura, we could see, was full of prickly sensations and dark colours. Our initial task was to gently question the lady to see if the phenomena were the product of her imagination.

'Watch your head as you go below,' said the lady's husband as he guided us aboard. Someone promptly banged his head. 'And watch yourself round here,' he said, as the same person banged himself again. We all chuckled. It was important to keep a cheerful, light-hearted spirit between ourselves as we prepared ourselves for the encounter.

We all squeezed around the table at the bow of the boat and settled down with a cup of tea. The atmosphere on board was odd, but not as sinister as Jane and I were expecting. It was certainly a strange place to live, and not a place for those who loved their creature comforts. There was limited decoration, a lot of damp, and no space at all. It had a musty smell.

Once we had settled in, we all relaxed and tuned-in to spirit. We all agreed that John, the medium who first organized the clearance, would act as the leader of the group. His wife Ethel sat next to him, Jane and I sat together and Nick, the Spiritualist church member, sat opposite us. The husband and wife who owned the boat stood in the doorway to the side of us. The following prayer was said to ask for protection and for God to be with us with our work:

Father, may you give us the protection that we need with this work. Bring to us from spirit those guides and helpers that we each know and also those that come here to help with this type of work in particular.

May the higher angelic helpers be here with us also. Protect us in what we do and give your blessing to our task so that the troubles that fill this place may be lifted. Amen.

As the words of the prayer unfolded we could feel a strength and joy as the power of the spirit built around us to aid us with our work. The next step was to challenge the spirit to come forward. Like a snake under a dark rock, it had to be coaxed into the light and disarmed. The boat was still but some of the keys hanging on the wall on a nail swung a little. We all noticed it but continued as if nothing had happened: perhaps it was nothing.

'Come on, you coward,' said John in a loud stern voice. 'You've bullied this lady enough! Now there are five of us to take on. Come on, we challenge you to show yourself. Come out!'

Nothing happened. Again he made similar retorts. 'Come on, show yourself. You want to scare people, come and scare us!' Then we felt what can best be described as a thickening of the atmosphere and a feeling of someone standing close to us. I could feel the face of a man press close to mine, then leave me and go towards Jane, who described it as follows:

The man felt angry and very violent, yet at the same time he felt fright-ened and confused. I could tell that he didn't like women at all and that he felt it was bad luck that women should be on his boat. 'Get away from me,' I projected in my thoughts. 'Go and pick on a man, you bully, go and try and take on Nick from the church.'

As Jane sent these thoughts we all saw Nick's face change. He went bright red and he looked frightened.

'Who's he with now?' somebody asked aloud.

'He's with Nick, can't you see?' I said.

'That's right, he's over here with me,' said Nick. We all sent out our power to help Nick with his struggle. The spirit left him and I felt him draw close to me. I closed my eyes and said, 'There seems to be two of them, there's a little boy here with an angry man. Someone has been hit hard across the head with something heavy. That's one of the things that's making him so angry.'

'I felt it across my head as well,' said John, 'And me too,' said Ethel. 'He has a thing about women being on his fishing boat. It's bad luck!'

The spirit man's unexpressed anger at the time of his passing was holding him to this world. His death was linked somehow with a woman and he was taking it out on the lady who now lived on board. We all agreed that we were feeling the same sensations and description of the man in spirit. We countered his anger by all mentally projecting thoughts of love and encouragement for the trapped soul to progress onward to the spirit world.

'Come on now,' said John. 'Your time now is finished. It's time to go to the spirit world.' We felt the spirit moving between us. His aggression began to soften. I felt him leave Jane and the others and return to me. I could hear his voice clearly in my mind. 'I'll suffer for what I've done if I go over there' he said in a rough, rasping voice. 'They'll send me to hell for sure.' He drew closer still. I tried to reassure him that no God sat on a golden throne and no one was going to throw him into an eternal hell. God didn't want vengeance. He wanted only our love. Hadn't this man suffered enough by being bound by his anger to this world? He owed it to himself and the young boy who clung to him to seek God's unceasing forgiveness. He had as much right as anybody to enter the kingdom of heaven, his own conscience would be the judge of his soul.

As each of us reaffirmed these ideas in our own way we could feel the spirit man's grip begin to loosen. We all sensed him crying. He let go.

The ecstasy in his soul was contagious. As he departed I had a beautiful vision of a great staircase leading up through the clouds with angels of light standing at the sides. I could see the man's silhouette, small and dark against this heavenly setting. I was seeing that man's image of heaven as he left this earth. Perhaps when I die I will have a different passing vision, but what I saw that night was quite beautiful. Another soul had found peace.

The heavy atmosphere had left the room as we all started to return to normal consciousness. The suffocating atmosphere had gone. 'He's gone now,' Jane said to the lady. 'Can you feel the difference in this place?' The boat was, as far as we know, never troubled again.

Case File 5

The people who approach Jane and I come from all walks of life. We have seen doctors, solicitors, businessmen, and even a High Court judge. But when a psychiatrist telephoned and asked for assistance I was very surprised – normally they reject mediums out of hand.

Warminster-based psychiatrist Dr Medway contacted me and asked if I could visit a patient's home to find out if it really was haunted. She explained, 'The lady involved is convinced that she is under a ghostly attack. She insists that a poltergeist is throwing things around the room and that a shadowy man is trying to attack her.'

We visited the house together, hoping to convince the lady that there was nothing to worry about. But when we stepped into the living room we all saw a strange white mist that clung to the floor. It was clear that we were dealing with something real after all.

The lady showed me around the house and I sat and meditated at the places where, she said, the manifestations were strongest. I described a bearded man who was troubling her. The description fitted what she had been seeing. The spirit told me that he was a gypsy and that he was buried nearby. I talked to him calmly and after a long and difficult inner debate he agreed to go. The psychiatrist looked as relieved as everyone else.

When the records were checked it was found that gypsies had camped extensively in that area many years ago. They had no formal cemetery but it was believed that they buried their dead in the vicinity of the house, in the woods that had once covered the estate.

Case File 6

It appears that many of the spirits that become trapped on the earth plane have worries about their place of burial. One example is Julie Benyan's experience of a recurring ghost. The family live in adjoining cottages.

> Problems mainly occur in Granddad's house. Sometimes there's a mysterious burning smell that's followed by a rap on the door. Nobody is ever there. The whole family have heard unexplained footsteps and we often hear loud raps from the coal house.

Julie believes that two ghosts haunt the house. They researched its 100-year history and found out about a epileptic boy whose parents used to lock him away for days in the coal house.

> This may account for the coal house rappings. But we also learned that a terrible murder took place here in Victorian times and a body was buried in a ditch outside. The murder is still unsolved, so perhaps the ghost is still trying to communicate and tell us what happened.

In the following case Beverley and her family were at first scared of their ghost but now treat her as a family friend:

> All our family have seen the little Victorian girl who wears a long night dress – we have called her Emily. I asked the previous owners of the house if they'd seen anything and they exclaimed 'Oh, she's back again, is she?'

Jane was the first to investigate Beverley's story.

> I told Beverley that I was receiving psychic impressions of a blue patterned jug and a dog's bones that had been buried in the garden. I then felt drawn to a particular spot near a tree in the garden. 'This is where Emily's dog was buried,' I said, pointing to the ground. 'And it is here that you also found the blue jug.'

Beverley confirmed that bones and blue china had been found where Jane said. Jane now knew that the spirit of Emily was real. Jane said that the girl had died in a well that had recently been covered over. They later checked the records and found this to be true – beneath the new kitchen were the remains of an old well.

When I investigated the cottage Emily told me about a St Christopher medal the owners had found under a tile in the kitchen. I pointed to the stone tile and they confirmed that this was the exact place it was found. Beverley rummaged through a draw and handed me the St Christopher to help me build my link with the spirit by holding it.

Emily took me on a tour round her old home. She was aware that she was dead, but preferred to stay put, so long as nobody minded. It was her that had been trying to draw attention to herself by moving the children's toy clowns and, as described and witnessed by Beverley, making them come 'alive'. Beverley had decided to burn the offending clowns in the garden. 'There was a piercing scream as I threw them on the bonfire,' said Beverley. 'It nearly scared the life out of me.' Emily was sorry that she had scared them all.

Jane had assessed the situation correctly when she had visited earlier. She had told the owners that Emily had fallen down the well when the authorities arrived to take her to a children's home after her parents died. Children's homes in Victorian times were fearsome places.

The spirit of Emily began telling me how the house had changed and the owner was able to confirm this. Strangely, one of the bedrooms had once been a larder and Beverley said that they'd had to completely strip this large room of wooden shelving and cupboards. The children's room, I said, had once been Emily's and this is where, I was told, she had most often been seen, dressed in her long white night dress.

There was one manifestation of Emily that had not been so pleasant. Beverley told me that on one of the walls on the house a mark had appeared and disappeared.

Emily led me into the living room and told me to place my hand on a particular place on the plain, clean wall. I turned to Beverley and said, 'Emily is telling me that it wasn't a simple mark that you saw here on the wall. It was the red hand of blood!' Emily had been so desperate to get their attention that she had resorted to these somewhat frightening manifestations.

Beverley looked shocked and I began to wonder if I had spoken out of turn. I didn't want to be alarmist but, although she had said nothing about this to anyone before, this is exactly what the whole family had seen at the place where I put my hand. They had been waiting to find out if I would spontaneously 'pick up' about the hand. It had naturally worried the family a great deal, and they were concerned that it was not the friendly spirit of Emily, but a sinister spirit that might do them harm. Fortunately, it was only Emily from the spirit side. Again I could feel her apologizing – she was sorry she'd scared them. Beverley says:

> Although some people would be worried by a ghost we feel that Emily is a nice spirit to have around. She's never given us any more trouble and the last thing we would want is for Craig and Jane to get rid of her.

Case File 8

This case really intrigued me, not only because a real ghost was involved, but because the whole family seemed to be so genuinely pleased to know that their house was haunted.

Nobody knows quite how old the traditional Somerset farmhouse of Willow Farm, adjoining the site of the annual Glastonbury Festival, is. Some of its stonework, and particularly the stone pillars by the fireplace, was retrieved from the ruins of Glastonbury Abbey that was destroyed by Henry VIII. Legend has it that long ago two brothers jointly inherited it but argued incessantly. Finally a blood bath took place within the house as one brother brutally murdered the other. Jane Fear, who together with her husband David, brought up her four children in the house, explains how 'the whole family is aware of our ghost'. It was Jane's eldest daughter, Sandra, who gave it the name Fred:

> Having a ghost around the house was part of our childhood. So many spooky things happened around our house that we all take it for granted. The strangest occurrence was when my brother Richard's bedroom door would open and we would hear footsteps cross the landing and walk down the stairs. When they reached the bottom we would see the stair door open by itself.
>
> When this happened, one of us would usually call out, 'Oh Fred, we do wish you'd learn to shut the door!'

Sandra's father, David, continues:

> We've had the occasional visitor be terrified by what happens. They have refused to stay in the house but we see no reason to worry. Fred's never hurt any of us and even our three dogs and three cats seem comfortable when he's around.

In 1976 the main beam of the house gave way and considerable work was undertaken to repair the house. Sandra again:

> We were all worried that Fred would either clear off or show his disapproval when the repairs were complete. Mum was really concerned. But within a few days we saw a shape at the top of the stairs and the doors and footsteps were soon back.

'I was overjoyed,' says Jane. 'It would have been awful to lose Fred – he's part of the family!' The Fear family certainly don't live up to their name. They take exactly the right attitude. Many people are absolutely terrified by the slightest creak or hint of a ghost. It is worth remembering that sometimes ghosts are just an atmosphere left in a building which replays itself like a video recording. Sometimes a spirit does get trapped between this world and the next but they are usually more frightened than we are. I'm sure that the attitude of the Fear family to Willow Farm's ghost will help Fred to progress toward the higher levels of the afterlife.

Case File 9

Another great story, involving a country ghost known as The Green Lady, was sent to me by Annette:

It was October 1954 and I was 24 years old. My glorious grandmother, whom I adored, was dying. I thought of her as I cycled home to Malmesbury on the road between Crudwell Village and Lord Suffolk's Estate. There were a couple of cottages to my right and opposite was a farm gateway. As I approached it I saw an apparition gliding about 4 feet up in the air and drifting towards the centre of the road.

It was a misty Sunday morning, so I assumed at first that it was the light playing tricks on me. I cycled up close and came face to face with the figure. It was a woman in a long brown coat. She had a featureless face with dark, empty sockets for eyes. Not knowing what to say or do I stuttered out the words 'Good morning'.

As I spoke, the silent figure floated slowly backwards into the gateway. I was more curious than frightened.

For years people laughed at me when I recalled this weird event. But my husband listened and, in 1963, soon after we were married, we visited the same place and asked at the cottages about the ghost. 'You saw the Green Lady who haunts that very spot!' replied the householder.

On the Tuesday after seeing the ghost my grandmother died.

Earthbound spirits

This final case file is a good example of what we call a ghost, phantom, apparition or spectre. Some people are mystified, intrigued, shocked or frightened when they 'see' this form of spontaneous phenomena.

Some scientists believe that the brain emits an electrical 'morphic field' that imprints itself on the environment. They argue that ghosts and apparitions are then seen when our psychic abilities read these mental recordings. Consequently the same ghostly figure is seen time and time again at the same place. In the last story the person seeing the ghost was fatigued from cycling, and her sensitivity at the time of her grandmother's illness probably opened her to these vibrations. Just as we would say that a photograph of a person is not the person themselves, so a ghost is likewise not a conscious being. It is a series of mental vibrations left in the atmosphere of the environment that a sensitive person can perceive unfolding like a film.

In the case of the teenage boys playing with the ouija board (Case File 1) it is debatable whether spirit forces were present at all. When a group of people gather to consciously manifest psychic phenomena they can tap into their own mental powers which influence and manipulate matter. Scientists call this power psychokinesis. When the young men assembled around the ouija board their thoughts may have blended together by telepathy. As they asked about the future, their subconscious fears were triggered and the result was the frightening prediction that became self-fulfilling.

In the stories about the haunted boat (Case File 4), the gypsy graveyard (Case File 5) and the Victorian child called Emily (Case File 7), I believe we are dealing with manifestations of conscious spirits that were earthbound. When the time of death comes, the spirit and the physical body part company. Manifesting in the etheric body the spirit goes on to a different dimension to our material world and joins the afterlife. Feelings, memories and personality are retained by the spirit.

Earthbound spirits are those that, for various reasons, still cling to our world. Often they do not even know that they are dead. An unresolved inner conflict, feelings of revenge, guilt or a desperate need to finish their earthly business stops them progressing. These spirits cannot hurt or harm anyone – they have no body to hurt you with – but may frighten some people. Mediums are trained to link with these entities who wish to make contact, and will reassure them and help them to move on. We will send out thoughts to direct the departed one towards other spirits who know and love them and together convince the earthbound spirit to enter the ever-forgiving afterlife.

Although it makes interesting reading, work with earthbound spirits is only a very tiny part of our work. Cases like these are extremely rare. The main thrust of our mediumistic work is to communicate with the spirit people who return from the bliss of the afterlife to reassure their loved ones on earth that they are happy, safe and well.

Chapter Seven

Celebrity Case Files

Most entertainers are creative, extrovert and sensitive – the same personality traits that paranormal researchers tell us make a good psychic. So it is no wonder that the superstars of the creative professions have paranormal tales to tell that are stranger than Hollywood fiction. Some claim to know the future, that they are in touch with the dead and even that they possess the power of spiritual healing.

For example, pop megastar Michael Jackson claims that he inwardly communicates with the flamboyant pianist Lee Liberace who died in 1987. Jackson reveals that, 'I have my own secret room, with a moving wall and mirrors. That's where I talk to Lee. His is the voice I hear in there. I feel his presence so very close to me.'[1] He adds that Liberace 'is like my guardian angel. He's even given me permission to record his theme song "I'll Be seeing You".'

Liberace also believed that at times he was paranormally inspired. He owned the piano which once belonged to the classical composer Liszt. 'When I play his compositions on it I have the most eerie feeling, as if I'd played that music before in another time.' And just like Liberace, Liszt was a flamboyant dresser.

Messages from beyond

Some stars of the music industry have deliberately sought the advice of the spirit world. Rock star Roger Daltry of The Who says he spoke with the band's former drummer Keith Moon, who died of a drug overdose in 1978. 'I've spoken to Keith, or rather to his spirit,' says Daltry. 'There's a psychic woman I go to see who doesn't know who I am or who Keith is.'[2]

Pop star Neil Tennant, from the Pet Shop Boys, also spoke to the dead and saw his future with the ouija board:

> It happened when I was 15. A group of us decided to have a seance, and we got in touch with the ghost of Oscar Wilde. He warned us not to make the same mistakes that he did. He told me I would be famous one day.[3]

Neil was pleased with the news from spirit. 'It was the advice I was longing for. Ever since I was a young lad, I desperately wanted to be a pop star.'

Creative people often have latent powers and are more inclined to see spirits and ghosts. Mick Jagger, lead singer of The Rolling Stones, was spooked by a bell-ringing eighteenth-century ghost when house hunting at a £3.5 million Gothic mansion. Housekeeper Anna-Maria Sliwinski told reporters:

> He seemed to change his mind rather suddenly after we told him about the ghost. I have heard the ghost first-hand. I heard strange chimes on a windless night. The bells were ringing in the tower, but there was nobody else in the house.[4]

Filmstar Dan Ackroyd even claims to be haunted by his best friend, and co-star in the film *The Blues Brothers*, John Belushi, who died of a drug overdose in 1982. He claims to see Belushi in Studio 8H where they worked together. 'It's weird,' says Ackroyd. 'It's as if John is trapped in limbo there.'[5]

Singer and television star Cilla Black knows what it's like to share a house with a ghost and has often seen the spectre of a girl by her bed. 'She's appeared to me loads of times,' Cilla says. 'She's about 14 with a sweet, sensitive face that has a really sad expression. I had this strong feeling she was searching for someone.'[6] Researchers revealed that a man called Thomas Redley once lived in Cilla's house in Buckinghamshire, England. His wife died suddenly and, soon after, Thomas died of a heart attack. Their daughter Lillian was left in the house alone. Three years later she died from pneumonia, aged 13.

The ghost of Lillian appears to be quite friendly, but the same cannot be said of so the poltergeist that haunts the house of pop star and actor Sting, who described a mysterious power that sent a razor-sharp knife flying across his kitchen:

> It propelled itself over the room and embedded itself into a wall. Just before that, the mobiles in my daughter's bedroom began to spin crazily although there was no one in the room at all. Even all the windows were tightly closed so there could be no draught whatsoever.[7]

Sting or his daughter, or both, were probably displaying the powers of psychokinesis which is defined as the power of the mind to influence matter. This psychic energy can move objects and in some people manifests as a spiritual healing power.

Spiritual healing

Liberace believed he had healing powers, having once said, 'Why, the other day, in the Hollywood Bowl two cripples arose and walked at my command. I said to them, "If you really want to walk for me, you can!" So they did.'[8]

Soccer legend Pelé – hailed as the greatest footballer ever – says he can cure cancer-stricken children and help crippled youngsters walk again. He told Brazilian *Playboy* magazine that he performs miracles when parents ask him to visit their children.

> Those children are in wheelchairs. Miraculously, when I touch them they start walking again – my God! I visit them in hospital and the boys and girls are cured. Parents call me saying their kid has one month to live. I go to the hospital and the kid recovers.[9]

Many stars have experimented with spiritual healing during illness. Michael Bentine, voice of the 1950s' British radio comedy *the Goons Show* fought a long battle with bone cancer with the help of spiritual healers. Bentine's father was a psychic researcher and it is not surprising that his son should follow in his father's footsteps.

Film star Omar Sharif was more sceptical. While filming in Bulgaria he was doubled over with pain because of a stomach ulcer. Then the producer's wife, actress Betty Bolvary, told him that she was a spiritual healer.

'At first I scoffed at her,' admitted Omar, 'but she insisted, asking me to give her just one minute. Gripped by pain, I thought, "What will one minute cost me?" So I agreed.'[10] After Betty had finished, Omar had changed his tone. 'I realized in that moment that the pain had gone. There was not even the slightest twinge. In 60 seconds I had been cured.'

Many psychics and healers believe that crystals, particularly quartz, can amplify healing energies. It has been claimed that Elizabeth Taylor's persistent health problems may be caused by her love affair with overpowerful diamonds. Crystals are said to have protective properties as well.

Actor Michael York is a firm believer in ESP and takes an interest in the New Age Movement that is spearheaded in the United States by actress Shirley Maclaine. He believes that a pocketful of crystals saved his life when six thugs attacked him and his wife in Rio de Janeiro. The actor went to defend himself and, to his amazement, the muggers fled. He is convinced that the crystals, which were given to him by a Brazilian healer, protected him.[11]

Gloria Swanson, who passed away in 1983, also accepted the reality of spiritual healing. 'I have seen healer Miss Kuhlman cure dozens of people of many different illnesses,' she said when interviewed by American broadcaster Bryce Bond. 'I have seen little children become hysterical with joy when their mothers or fathers suddenly walked after years of being crippled.'[12] She also said, 'I accept the afterlife's reality,' and described how once she left her physical body and 'went a few blocks away'.

Power travel

Many psychics believe it is possible to leave the physical body or clairvoyantly witness events occurring at another place. The American chat show hostess Joan Rivers has claimed to have travelled out of her body. She says that she 'flew' to California, where her daughter lived. 'I saw my daughter in the shower – I rang immediately to confirm what happened – and that's exactly what she had been doing.'[13]

Mediums, like myself, believe that at physical death the spirit leaves the body to enter the afterlife. But that's not the end of the story. The people we love can return to guide and inspire us through our intuition. Hollywood heart-throb and star of the hit film *Ghost* Patrick Swayze, says he is frequently visited by the spirit of his father who passed in 1982. 'He appears in my dreams as an old Indian warrior. We were so close. I still want to cry every time I think of him,'[14] the star comments.

Jane Fonda, daughter of late film star Henry Fonda, also claims her father's spirit visits her. Jane says of her famous dad, who passed away in 1982, 'I welcome the interest he takes in my work. After all, if anyone should know about the movie business it's Henry Fonda.'[15]

Premonitions

Many people get a psychic flash of foreboding that can sometimes save a life. Actors and actresses are no exception. Actor David Niven's wife,

Hjordis, had a premonition that she would be accidentally shot. No one believed her even though twelve guests at a shooting party heard her commenting on it.

'Sure enough,' said one guest, 'our host didn't see her standing behind a bush and accidentally shot her. Fortunately she was at the edge of the pattern of shot so she was not killed. Hjordis got 30 shots in her.'[16]

Singer Eartha Kitt believes that her ESP gifts are a 'strange power which can suddenly warn something bad will happen to someone very close to me.'[17] In 1965, whilst visiting Argentina, she sensed that something was terribly wrong with her three-year-old daughter, so she took the first flight back home to Los Angeles. 'I hurried home to hear my daughter cry, "Mommy, I'm so sick". She had a temperature of 103 and was rushed to hospital where she fully recovered.'

Eartha's warnings have proved correct in several instances. When, in 1955, she greeted her best friend James Dean, Eartha told him 'Your body is here, but your spirit isn't.'[18] The young actor passed seven days later in a car crash. Similarly, actress Ursula Andrews didn't like the vibrations she felt from his car. She said, 'I told him the car gave me a bad feeling. He promised to be careful and said goodbye. I knew I would never see him again.'[19]

Many famous stars have believed in an afterlife or had premonitions of their death. Elvis Presley said that he believed he would die when he saw pictures in cumulus clouds that predicted his death. John Lennon, of the Beatles, took an active interest in Spiritualism and attended many seances with his wife Yoko Ono. It is believed that John had a premonition that he would be shot. He even stated that his fear of murder caused the Beatles to break up, saying, 'We were not bored, and certainly did not run out of songs. I was paranoid about somebody trying to bump us off.'[20] When he heard that the Beatles' road manager had been shot dead by Los Angeles police, he said over and over again, 'I'm next, I know it.' John believed firmly in an afterlife, and said, 'I am an optimist about eternity. I believe in life after death. I believe that death is not an end but a beginning.'

Spirits on the world stage

Many world leaders are deeply interested in the paranormal and ESP, and their beliefs may have influenced their military decisions. President Jimmy Carter believes he saw a UFO, and Ronald and Nancy Reagan's interest in astrology has been well reported. Biographer Kitty Kelly claims in *Nancy Reagan – The Unauthorized Biography* [21] that when Reagan became California's governor in the late 1960s he took his oath of office in the middle of the night, 'acting on advice from an astrologer who said that this was the most propitious time'.

Kelly also claims that the Reagans 'were devoted clients of Carroll Righter, a Los Angeles astrologer, and secret devotees of Jean Dixon, a "seer"'. It is claimed by many sources that Reagan always consulted the stars before making his decisions – a tradition that Hillary Clinton is said to be maintaining.

Soviet President Mikhail Gorbachev's paranormal interests are less well documented. However, it was alleged that, before he fell from power, he smuggled a blind clairvoyant called Vanga into the Kremlin so she could 'read' sugar cubes for him. The troubled Soviet leader was said to have 'quizzed her for two hours on his future' [22] before flying her home to Bulgaria in a government aircraft. When questioned about the incident, a Kremlin spokesman tactfully replied, 'It's no secret that Gorbachev has been under immense strain recently and this prompted his actions.' Considering the events that were to take place the following year, I expect that Vanga's predictions were far from sweet.

In Britain, it was Queen Elizabeth I (1533–1603) who first made major political decisions based on the evidence of 'seers'. Her clairvoyant advisor, John Dee, prophesied the attempted invasion of England by the Spanish Armada in 1588 and the execution of Mary Queen of Scots in 1587.

World War II

Paranormal beliefs had enormous influence on strategic decisions and world events during World War II. Hitler, Himmler, Goering, Rosenberg and Goebbels were all interested in the occult and this is well documented. Hitler was born in Braunauam-Inn, Austria – a place known for its seers and magic traditions. As a young man he was taught to develop his psychic abilities by Professor Haushofer, and later in Vienna attended numerous lectures about numerology, graphology, water divination, astrology, psychokinesis and physiognomy. One of his early associates said that Hitler believed that he could detect Jews by dowsing over them with a pendulum and the Nazis applied phrenology in an attempt to determine who had Slav, Jewish, Bolshevik or Aryan skulls.

A distorted version of the prophecies of Nostradamus, who predicted the rise of an anti-Christ called Hister, was used by the Nazis for propaganda, and Hitler consulted his own personal astrologer, Karl Ernst Kraft, when making major military decisions. Realizing that Hitler's war strategy was being influenced by metaphysical considerations, Churchill in turn employed his own astrologers to ascertain what decisions Hitler was likely to make based upon the movements of the planets.

Winston Churchill possessed a natural psychic gift himself that saved his life many times. In his autobiography *My Early Life* [23] he says that in his youth he had held a planchette 'and written while others had touched (his) wrist or hand'. He also tells of how in the Boer War, when working as a reporter for the *Morning Post*, his train was ambushed and he was confined to a prison camp. He escaped into territory unknown to him and says that his intuition guided him to knock recklessly on the door of a house and reveal that he was British. 'Thank God you have come here,' cried the stranger, 'it is the only house where you would not have been handed over. But we are all British here.'

His life was saved again when fighting in World War I on the western front. While he was making his report to the general, his dugout was blown up. He later said, 'And then there came the sensation that a hand had been stretched out to move me in the nick of time from a fatal spot.' During the Blitz, clairvoyance saved his life again. Churchill always sat in the same seat in his car but one night suddenly decided to change his routine. A bomb landed nearby and he would have been killed if he hadn't made this impulsive seating decision. When his wife asked him why he had made the change, he said, 'Something said to me "Stop!" before I reached the car door held open for me. It then appeared to me I was meant to open the other side and get in and sit there – and that's what I did.'

In 1940 he again sensed danger and in his mind's eye 'saw' the huge windows at Horse Guards Parade, which backs onto the seat of British government at 10 Downing Street, being smashed. He ushered everyone to safety three minutes before splintering glass sprayed the building.

Churchill believed in destiny and that some invisible power guided his life. 'I have the feeling that we have a Guardian because we serve a great cause, and that we shall have that Guardian so long as we serve that cause faithfully.'

Across the ocean in America, Franklin D. Roosevelt was also being guided by spirits. There is evidence to suggest that he attended seances. A 1944 edition of *Chimes* magazine said that he and some of his cabinet 'secured very good mediums, held many seances and listened carefully to suggestions made by former presidents, generals, admirals and diplomats now residing in the spirit world'.

In Canada, William Lyon Mackenzie King, who was Prime Minister 1935–48 (he died in 1950), was also consulting the dead. He made no secret about this to his intimate friends, some of whom joined his seances in his library at home. King used both the crystal ball and a ouija board and his diaries reveal that he experienced visions and prophetic dreams. On his deathbed heads of state gathered to meet him, including King George VI, Churchill, Pandit Nehru and two strange, unknown women. The two women sat with him for 50 minutes as he made his preparations to die. They were Geraldine Cummins and Miss Gibbes – an Irish medium and her companion.

In Russia, Stalin was also taking an interest in the paranormal. When he heard of the astonishing psychic abilities of the Polish Jew Wolf Messing he decided to meet him. The perplexed Messing was arrested and questioned by Stalin himself about the destiny of Russia.

Stalin decided to put Messing to the test. He was to undertake a 'psychic bank robbery' and take 100,000 roubles from the Moscow Gosbank, where he was unknown. Wolf Messing could use his telepathic powers to hypnotize. He walked into the bank and handed the cashier a blank sheet of paper and was immediately given the money he wanted. Two of Stalin's official witnesses confirmed to their leader what had happened. When the cashier realized that he was holding a blank sheet of paper he fainted with shock.

As if this wasn't enough, Stalin demanded that Messing undertake another impossible task. He took Messing to a secure government building and personally ordered three guards to watch him, insisting that Messing, under no circumstances, should leave the building. Messing succeeded again and cheekily waved goodbye to a high government official looking out of one of the windows.

Stalin still wasn't satisfied. Messing had to risk his life again. He was ordered to illegally enter Stalin's heavily guarded country house. Messing used mental suggestion to convince the guards and servants that he was really Lavrenti Beria – the head of the secret police – even though he bore no physical resemblance to him. Once again he triumphed.

Stalin was now so impressed that, as a reward, he granted Messing permission to tour freely throughout the Soviet Union – he could probably have used his psychic powers to do that anyway!

Finally, even the devout Roman Catholic French general and statesman Charles de Gaulle joined in paranormal pursuits during World War II. When France fell to the Nazis he fled to England to lead the Free French fighting forces. Here he consulted the British medium Bertha Harris, whom he met at a country house party. The other guests included Winston Churchill and King George of Greece – a firm believer in Spiritualism.

Bertha predicted that de Gaulle would liberate France, and that he would become its leader. The prophecy was fulfilled. Charles de Gaulle led the French troops into Paris in June 1944 and later became the first president of the Fifth Republic.

1. *Psychic News*, 14 February 1987.
2. *Psychic News*, 28 August 1993.
3. *Psychic News*, 13 April 1991.
4. Francis Marshall, *Living With Spirits*, Harlequin Books.
5. *Psychic News*, 25 September 1993.
6. *Daily Star*, 19 February 1993; from Francis Marshall, *Living With Spirits*, Harlequin Books.
7. Francis Marshall, *Living With Spirits*, Harlequin Books.
8. *Psychic* News, 14 February 1987.
9. From *Playboy* magazine.
10. *Psychic News*, 26 December 1987.
11. Reported in the *Daily Star*, 19 February 1993.
12. *Psychic News*, 27 February 1988.
13. Julie Byron, *Amazing Psychic Experiences of the Famous*.
14. *Psychic News*, 23 December 1995.
15. *Psychic News*, 23 December 1995.
16. *Psychic News*, 26 December 1987.
17. *Psychic News*, 2 January 1988.
18. Julie Byron, *Amazing Psychic Experiences of the Famous*.
19. *Psychic News*, 26 December 1987.
20. *Psychic News*, 2 January 1988.
21. Published by Pocket Books, 1992.
22. *Psychic News*, 9 June 1990.
23. Published by Simon and Schuster, 1930.

Chapter Eight
Taking Flight

Many people claim that during sleep they step out of their body and travel around strange, new worlds. These 'dreams' are unlike normal sleep for the person feels as if they are completely lucid and 'awake' when they happen. It is a very common occurrence and you may have even experienced it yourself. Reports of 'out-of-body experiences' (OBEs) suggest to many scientists that awareness is not dependent upon the brain but can exist independently. In this chapter you will read about people who have found themselves floating on the ceiling, have temporarily stepped into the afterlife, or have come back from other dimensions to bring us messages of hope and reassurance.

Case File 1

During a public demonstration I received a message for someone named Jenny who was linked with the surname Mathews. Jenny Perrin takes up the story:

> Craig said, 'This was a recent passing. It is a young, somewhat rebellious man who died before his time'. Another lady in the audience thought it was for her, but Craig soon understood that he was on the wrong link. He realized that the message was meant for me. I took the surname to be of nineteen-year-old Brett Mathews – a very close friend who had died a few months ago. We had known each other since early childhood and were like a brother and sister. I was still suffering from the shock of his sudden and tragic passing.
>
> Craig explained that Brett was a soul who was not meant to reside on earth for a long time. Everybody complained that he had died before his time, but really he had come home; he loved his new life in the afterlife.

'He's explaining the way he died,' continued Craig. 'It was pitch black when the tragedy happened. Something hit him so hard from behind that it even broke the sternum of his chest. Others were with him when it happened. They were carrying lights. I believe that he's telling me that he was struck from behind by a train.'

Craig had got it right. This was exactly what had happened on that fateful night.

Craig continued by describing some of the other things that Brett was showing him: how he continually ate chewing gum and couldn't stand still, rode a bike, had a recent girlfriend called Joe, how he cheated at cards and that he had got the letter from his friend Peter. Craig also said that Brett was talking about someone called Keith Jenkins who was grieving for him. He mentioned the games we played as children and how we used to own an oil lamp with a picture on the front of it and a strange roof-like shape on the top. As children we also adopted a Jack Russell dog. He gave the birthday dates of 14 June and 9 September as being significant.

Craig had again got it right but was wrong with the birthdays; then Brett never was much good at remembering birthdays. The numbers were the wrong way round: Brett's birthday was 14 September and mine was 9 June. Craig also kept saying that he could hear the word 'Street' but couldn't hear the place name before it. 'Street' wasn't a road at all. Brett must have been trying to tell Craig about Kelly Street, one of his closest friends who was torn apart on hearing the news of the death.

Brett was trying to reassure us all that he was all right in the afterlife. Craig said that Brett's mum was taking his death very badly and he wanted her to know that he loved her. 'You've seen him twice yourself,' said Craig. 'On one occasion the door slammed and he says, in his own words, that it scared the shit out of you!'

That's just how Brett would have phrased it. I'd seen his figure in my bedroom twice and on the second occasion the wardrobe door closed by itself. I nearly leapt out of my skin.

Brett Mathews reassured his friends that he was all right, and told many things about his life. But he left out an important fact in his communication. Private Brett Mathews, of the First Battalion Devon and Dorset Regiment based in North Germany, had died courageously. The incident had happened on a Monday in January during night manoeuvres. One of his comrades had got his foot caught in the railway line and it was Brett who had sacrificed his own life trying to save the life of his friend. There will always be a place in heaven for heroes.

Jenny's mother, Linda Perrin, had only just started taking an interest in Spiritualism. She goes on:

We didn't expect that evening also to get a message from our close friend Martin Cooper, but when Craig said that he had an impatient and quick-tempered man communicating with him and calling himself Cooper, I put my hand up. Nobody else could place the name so it appeared to be for me and Simon, who was sitting with me.

Craig continued by saying that Martin had thrown all of his money away before he died. He said that Martin never believed in an afterlife when he was alive and that he was now saying, 'Tell her there's no such thing as the afterlife! I still don't believe in it – even though I'm dead!' Of course, he was making his own silly jokes – he just didn't like to be proved wrong. His death, he told Craig, had been sudden, and he had died in a shop doorway. He had fallen to the floor, banging his head as he did so.

Martin had been a drug addict. He spent everything he had on drugs, sold all of his possessions and ended up on the street. Despite everyone's efforts, and believe me he was loved by many people, there was nothing we could do – he hated himself and was determined to destroy himself. His body was found in a shop doorway. His head was bruised.

Craig went on to describe Martin's other physical ailments correctly, such as the arthritis in his right hand, his stomach condition, and that he had a fear of cancer of the stomach. Martin mentioned the watch that his friend Melanie had. It wasn't working. (We checked this out later and the watch had broken down a couple of days before.)

Craig described what Martin's mother was like, and said that Martin wanted to let everyone know that he is all right now. 'Stop worrying and know that I'm happy in the next world.' Craig said that there was a lady in Lancashire who still hadn't heard the bad news yet. Her grief was to come. (A very close friend of Martin's lived in Lancashire, but was still away on holiday in Tenerife. She hadn't heard the news.) 'Also', said Craig, 'he's telling me to make sure that his scrappy dog is looked after.' Martin and his girlfriend, Jean, had a poodle dog whose coat had got very untidy. Jean had given the dog away to friends.

We all really sat up when Craig concluded his communication. 'They're shaving me,' Craig said that Martin was telling him. 'Just a minute – he says that they're shaving him right now. At this very moment. He's not been buried yet! His body's still in the morgue!'

There is no way that anybody could have known this. Martin had only died the day before and they were preparing Martin's body as Craig spoke.

At the time of death the 'astral body', which is like a body of light, leaves the physical body and ascends to one of the heavenly planes. It is unusual for the spirit person to be able to communicate so clearly after the time of death, although I have interviewed many people who say they have seen the recently deceased soon after they have passed over, and even attending their own funeral!

Many doctors are convinced that there is a consciousness that can exist separately to the physical body. When some of their patients come close to death, or have a traumatic accident, they give descriptions afterwards of leaving the physical body and observing what is taking place in other locations. The next case file is a good example.

Case File 2

What started as a family outing, shopping for antiques, became a nightmare for pregnant Melissa Pauper and her family. As her husband, Richard, drove her and their ten-year-old daughter Samantha back to their home, they were involved in a head-on collision. The combined speed of impact when the two cars collided was the equivalent of hitting a solid brick wall at 85 mph. All three passengers were left unconscious and trapped within the crumpled car. It took over two hours for the fire brigade to cut them out. Melissa continues:

Immediately after the impact everything went totally quiet and calm and we all became aware of being engulfed in a soothing yet brilliant ice blue light. It seemed to surround the whole car. Even though I had multiple injuries – I'd broken my sternum and fractured my spine – I felt nothing. Richard had gone through the windscreen and Samantha had serious head injuries. There was so much carnage that, as far as I knew, everyone was dead.

I then found myself outside of my body and sitting at the side of the road on a low flint wall. The wall was like a divide. Behind me was this beautiful green field. There were no trees, just a big, green plain as far as the eye could see. It was so peaceful, so beautiful. In the field I could see people. They were of all ages and all dressed in white. I could see children playing. Everyone was laughing and joking. The sky was clear blue and cloudless.

In front of me, on the other side of the wall and where the accident had happened, there was no colour at all. As I looked in the car I could only see Richard. It was as if I was standing back, watching someone else's accident.

Then, out of the blue light, stepped a petite old lady and a grey-haired old gentleman. I felt that I knew them somehow. They put their arms out. 'Join us. Come and join us,' they said. I had an overwhelming urge to follow them into the beautiful green field.

But a voice pulled me back with a jolt. 'Mummy, don't go!' It was Sam. As soon as she called me there was a painful wrench and I was pulled off the wall and into a tunnel. Suddenly I was back in the car and in a lot of pain.

Afterwards Samantha told me that she had also stepped out of her body, but couldn't get to the wall. She had been circling the car in a daze, then found herself back in her body and cried out to me. I wonder whether this is why I only could see Richard in the car when I 'saw' it.

As well as being worried for Sam and Richard, I was of course also worried for my unborn baby. We had been trying for so long to conceive and we'd made all the preparations and had started buying baby things. As I drifted in and out of consciousness in the ambulance I was visited by another spirit person, a small bald-headed man in a tweed coat and round glasses. He looked at me with a knowing smile and laid his hand upon my tummy. I understood at that moment that he had come to take the soul of the baby into his keeping but that she would be given back to me.

Four months later, Melissa lost the baby and was told that because of her injuries she could never again have children.

I was devastated by the news, as the thought of having a baby was keeping me going, but part of me never gave up hope. I remembered the angelic spirit messenger who told me that the child I would lose would be given back.

On Christmas Day 1995 she fell pregnant and on 27 September 1995 gave birth to Annabella:

Bella is a very spiritual child. It's like she's been here before. She wakes up laughing, rarely cries and is happy all the time. If any person can read my thoughts, it is her. If I want her to put something down that she's not allowed to play with, she'll drop it as soon as I send her the thought.

The accident has awakened something inside of me. I was always a little bit psychic, but now these powers have become very strong. It's taught me that material things are unimportant and that what really matters is life and people. I am now more aware of other people's feelings and have an uncanny knack of being able to anticipate people's thoughts and feelings. I'll just come out with things and they'll be right.

The most remarkable psychic talent that Melissa has learned from her ordeal is that she can now step in and out of her body at will.

I can astral travel deliberately. If I lose something, I'll sit down and relax and be taken straight to it. For example, the other day I lost my watch. I sat down, relaxed, then found myself behind the wardrobe in the bedroom. When I went and checked, there was the watch exactly where I had 'seen' it.

Near-death experiences

Studies led by researchers such as Michael B. Sabom, Elisabeth Kübler-Ross and Raymond Moody, of testimonials from hospital patients who have been snatched from the brink of death demonstrate that many people report similar experiences – they step outside of their body into their astral form. From a vantage point, usually on the ceiling, they see their 'dead' body. Sometimes they recall, when resuscitated, seeing their operation in progress. They narrate details about the procedures that, without an extensive medical knowledge, they could never have known.

(Case File 9)

One of the most remarkable stories was told to me by Elizabeth Hyde. After a severe asthma attack she was rushed to hospital.

I vaguely recall waking in an oxygen tent and a lot of fuss going on around me. I don't know at what point I drifted out of my body, but I do know now that my heart stopped and I was rushed to the

Resuscitation Ward. I could see myself attached to a ventilator with lots of wires connected to me. I could see a doctor, two nurses and the bizarre sight of a man dressed in a bow tie and full evening suit!

Elizabeth then went into cardiac arrest, but witnessed the unfolding scene from outside her body.

I saw them all trying to restart my heart. I was in no pain and felt no difficulty with my breathing. I was an onlooker, so to speak, watching myself in the hospital bed.

We had no telephone at home and I saw the police bring my husband to the hospital. 'Is there any hope?' I heard him say. 'Very little,' replied the man in the evening suit. That was the only moment I felt unhappy.

I felt myself falling down a tunnel and saw my life flash before me like a rapid series of camera pictures. Suddenly I was standing and feeling wonderful with a sense of lightness and happiness, and I knew that I was surrounded by a great love. Added to this was a feeling of tranquillity. I felt so well it was wonderful!

I then found myself standing to one side of a small arched bridge. There were people singing, not hymns but a lovely song of joy. There were colours such as I have never seen. I wanted to join them, but thoughts of my husband stopped me. There were also things that I still wanted to do in life, such as have a baby – but it was so very, very tempting to cross.

Standing on the bridge was a Jewish man holding a cross. He 'spoke' to me telepathically and asked, 'Are you ready to cross?'. I recall saying, 'No, No, No!' and then I immediately returned to my body. I could now 'hear' conversations going on around me in the hospital. 'She's slipping away,' they said. But I knew that I would live and started fighting the ventilator to prove that I could breathe by myself. 'Why can't these people see I'm not going to die?'

After four days Elizabeth was detached from the ventilator, transferred to a recovery ward and gradually got well.

The man who previously wore the evening suit when I was in a coma was now in a doctor's white coat as he walked into the ward. I asked the nurse about him. 'He's the surgeon who performed a tracheotomy operation on you to try to save your life,' said the nurse. 'I know,' I replied, 'but why was he wearing a bow tie and evening suit?' The nurse was dumbstruck and then explained that they had to call him from a very important dinner engagement!

I did have a child – a son, Simon, who is now 27. The previous year I had lost a baby, but I know he lives on and one day I will see him. I know I am lucky to have had such a wonderful experience.

Simon describes the impact Elizabeth's experience has had on the family:

Perhaps psychic gifts run in our family. Mum and I will try to call each other at exactly the same time. I know that Mum's experience helped her when Dad died, as she is now convinced that there's an afterlife. As for me, I used to regularly see his spirit walk into my room when I was a little boy.

Elizabeth's story is one of the most amazing accounts of a near-death experience that I have ever been told. Sceptics will of course say that it is all hallucination, but how could she have possibly have known that her surgeon was wearing a bow tie and evening suit? She was in a coma and having a tracheotomy performed. Elizabeth also knew that it was the police that brought her husband to the hospital, as she overheard their conversation, and also knew that a doctor and two nurses tried to resuscitate her heart. I am intrigued by the fact that she was greeted into the afterlife by a Jewish man holding a cross. Perhaps this tells us that the afterlife is not the exclusive domain of any one religion.

Most of us have heard of the tunnel of light which many people on the brink of death have described. They are drawn through this after leaving the body and are met, on the other side, by radiant, angelic beings and by the 'dead' friends and relatives who they once knew and loved. However, they are barred from going further across a symbolic bridge, or through a gate or door, when a being, usually a loved one, tells them in gentle tones that it is not their time to die. They are instructed to return, a prospect that has little appeal, and find themselves instantly transported back to the pain of their earthly body. Having tasted the nectar of heaven and glimpsed the ineffable beyond, their life goes through a spiritual metamorphosis. The material world, to which they are bound, seems pale compared to the glories of heaven. They long to return to the ethereal place that is their true home.

Critics propose elaborate theories to dismiss these testimonials. They claim that such near-death experiences are actually the result of hallucinations created by the drugs used, the disassociation resulting from the firing of the brain's temporal lobes, the fantasies of a brain starved of oxygen, or the effects of the release of the brain's natural opium-like chemicals and the illusory visions created by left-hemisphere brain activity.

These theories are, in my opinion, inadequate. Often the patients are free of drugs which might induce hallucinations, and we still do not know the function of the brain's temporal lobes. Ingested opium does not automatically trigger an out-of-body experience and memory recall, and the brain, when starved of oxygen, is absent or at best fuzzy. Near-death experiences are always vivid, lucid and they change lives forever.

The evidence we have considered throughout this book points to the existence of the afterlife. When reports of near-death experiences, dreams and visions of the dying, age-old beliefs and religions, and the experiences of hypnotized subjects are all taken collectively, the evidence is overwhelming.

The philosophical principle of Occam's Razor proposes that, in explaining something, assumptions must not be needlessly multiplied – in other words, the simplest theory corresponds to reality. The opposing theories of a few sceptical scientists twist and turn and in some cases border on the ridiculous. There is as much evidence to support the existence of an afterlife as there is scientific evidence to support the theory of relativity. Scientists can accept relativity – it confirms their belief in a material universe – but talk of an afterlife seems to arouse deep-felt resentment, scorn and derision, much as Galileo's telescope did in the Catholic Church in the sixteenth century.

The science of consciousness

Early mediums believed that the afterlife had a physical reality made from Etheric Matter that encircled the earth in concentric spheres. This, they said, was like the matter of earth but vibrated at a much higher frequency. Just as microwaves and x-rays are invisible to our perceptions, so too this Etheric Matter is invisible to our eyes or scientific instruments. Some still argue today that this Etheric Matter exists, and point to the missing 'dark matter' that the mathematicians of cosmology say must be there but which just can't be found. If these mediums' theories are right, then science may one day provide the key to unlock the door between this world and the next.

I believe, as do many mediums, that the afterlife should be thought of as a level of consciousness. To prove it scientifically we need a new science: the science of consciousness. However, an empirical study of consciousness may be impossible. As the Zen masters believe, 'The mind is like a sword that cuts but cannot cut itself.'

But what is consciousness? Is it measurable? Does it have a substance? What is its relationship to the concept of the self? These questions are conceptual rather than empirical, as there is no way, as yet, to measure consciousness. Nobody knows what it is or even how to begin a systematic study of it. Other baffling questions are raised by a study of it. Are all living things conscious? Could a machine become conscious? Is an unborn baby conscious? Are we fully conscious or do we also have an unconscious? Is our consciousness dependent on the body? Is consciousness and self one and the same? And so on.

The light of consciousness is the most perplexing enigma of the universe. Being conscious as opposed to 'dead' is certainly important to us. As far as we know, it is nature's greatest achievement – unless it's possible for nature to evolve something even more baffling. (Indeed, perhaps it is *not* the ultimate achievement of evolution. Maybe there is a state of being or non-being that goes beyond consciousness and already exists or non-exists somewhere in the far flung dimensions.)

Psychologists say that we have an unconscious, and that the left and right hemispheres of the brain function very differently and display contrasting forms of awareness. Psychologists are generally agreed on this. But if just one experiment in telepathy or mediumship was accepted as fact by traditional science it would demonstrate that consciousness can exist independently of the brain. Consciousness would be proven to be independent of matter, and the brain and body would be seen to be the temporary housing of the spirit.

If you can accept, without having to depend on any faith, that the afterlife is a reality, then you must also accept that there is a purpose to life on earth. This temporal sphere is, in my opinion, just a stepping stone to something greater. Material possessions, power, position, status have little value in the plan of things: a shroud has no pockets. We are instead on a holy mission to discover our divinity – the treasure beyond the material that worm and moth cannot corrupt. The search takes place in this life and continues in the life to come.

We are born to this world because there are certain spiritual subjects that we are obliged to learn on our path to self-realization.

Here is the school where we take our lessons. For the advanced pupil the lessons are hard because they demand that we change ourselves, evolve spiritually and take personal responsibility for our actions and destiny.

Our teachers are many but the greatest of them all is suffering. A spirit forged between the hammer and the anvil in the fires of adversity grows great. The poet William Blake expressed this in a beautiful way in his *Auguries of Innocence* c. 1803: 'Man was made for joy and woe, and if this we rightly know, then safely through the world we go.' In other words, it is through joy, suffering and acceptance that we learn our spiritual lessons. To free ourselves from attachment – and earth is the place where the forces of craving are most pronounced – brings liberation. To be free is to learn to love unreservedly. To fly we must let go.

The soul's journey

Some of life's lessons appear so brutal and unfair. For example, how wrong it appears that a baby who dies only weeks after its birth should have such a limited experience of this world. If this life is the place where we learn the lessons to prepare us for the next, then that child is going on to the next world disadvantaged. Surely they would get a second chance to learn the experiences available through life? This is one of the many reasons why Jane and I accept that reincarnation is part of the cosmic plan. Many mediums do not believe in reincarnation – they say that it is unproved – although numerous spirit teachers, who have spoken through famous trance mediums, say the soul takes on many incarnations.

Reincarnation explains why some people suffer and others have an easy life. To be born into a comfortable life does not necessarily mean that the person involved is worthy, or those that suffer do so because of evil deeds done in previous lives. Everyone has different lessons to learn from life.

For some, wealth brings suffering and for others, poverty brings spiritual growth. This world is the testing ground for the soul and each of us has a unique, custom-made examination to pass or fail. We return again and again until we have fully understood the lessons and changed ourselves accordingly.

The next incarnation is not instantaneous. We spend some time on earth and also time in the afterlife. When we are spiritually ready to learn new lessons we are reborn, together with those who are part of our 'group soul' who will become our friends and family in our new earth life. The group soul consists of those who are bound together spiritually by a common love and destiny. They are the people on earth whom you instinctively love. There are other members of our group soul who do not join us this time around – you are yet to meet some of your oldest friends.

Latent in our soul are the buried memories of past lives and of our time already spent in the afterlife. According to the Greek myth, we pass across the river Styx and forget our previous lives, in order that we can experience the world anew. But one day we will remember.

A simplistic description of the afterlife would be of a world very much like this one, where we spend an eternity under pleasant circumstances. This 'tea and biscuits in heaven' ideal is rejected by many thoughtful mediums. Like this world, the spirit planes are temporary places of residence. The first planes of afterlife existence are similar to this world but there are worlds within worlds in the beyond. Advanced souls, who have understood the illusionary nature of earthly existence, will, when they pass over, enter quickly into the higher more abstract states of consciousness. It all depends on the discarnate individual's level of understanding.

Entry into the afterlife is experienced in terms we can readily understand. We experience a world that is a perfected version of earthly life. Our soul is free of the restraints of the physical body and we see this level of reality in its full splendour. It is a world that is more beautiful than our own and many souls will continue at this level until it is time to take on another earthly incarnation.

Some souls will continue to live and experience a similar life to the one they knew on earth. Although they have no physical body they may continue to eat food or live in houses and do their chores such as housework, driving a car or perhaps even visiting the launderette! Gradually they may understand that their activities are illusionary habits. As their understanding of the nature of the afterlife increases they will become less dependent on the old earthly behaviour patterns and embrace a more fluid state of being.

When mediums communicate with the afterlife, it is from these first planes, which are closest to earthly existence, that the spirit makes his or her communication. Also, from both Jane's and my experiences, the communicating spirit's personality deviates little from the traits they exhibited on earth. Stubborn and swearing Uncle Frank often swears and puts forward his bigoted views even when he's gone to heaven. Some express their guilt concerning their earthly behaviour, but the personality itself doesn't seem to change a great deal. They become more aware of themselves but do not suddenly become enlightened.

The afterlife, I believe, is made of 'mindstuff' – that is, consciousness. It is a plane of 'being'. When a person enters the afterlife they take with them the sum total of their understanding. Most people comprehend the world to be something 'out there' and that the external world is real. This way of perceiving is taken with them on to the next planes of being and they experience the afterlife in terms that they are used to and understand. Consequently, they enter a world that is very much like this one with towns, countryside, skies and houses. Also they experience the afterlife within the cultural context that they knew on earth. Hence a Westerner will see Western-style civilization.

The major difference between this world and that of the afterlife is that the entrant is now free of the physical body and can experience reality without the constraints of the brain. The author Aldous Huxley thought of the brain as a reducing valve, a prison, that blocks the true perception of reality. He took mind-expanding drugs, such as mescaline, to open his perceptions and allow him to see the world in its 'naked existence'. Huxley's ecstatic, psychedelic visions were probably similar to the world we will see with our celestial eyes in the afterlife: incandescent, alive, vibrant and beautiful beyond words. We will see reality in its primal form.

Mediums communicate with the afterlife and assimilate information that we pass on to our sitters. Together with our own direct visionary experiences we are able to build a picture of what the next world is like. Much of what we have to say, and what other mediums have said in the past, is similar to the reports of people who have had a near-death experience. For the spirit communicator it must be like trying to explain colour to a person born blind – impossible to describe unless you have seen it for yourself. There is one thing of which you can be sure. One day you will see it for yourself.

Angels and spirit guides

Mediums believe that their work is guided by spiritually advanced beings from the higher realms of the afterlife planes. Like the Bodhisattvas from the Buddhist tradition, they return from the bliss of exalted consciousness to teach their message of love to the rest of us. When the medium enters a trance these spirit guides are able to communicate with us directly through the mouthpiece of the medium.

I first became aware of my spirit guides as a 19-year-old man, and the spiritual bond between us was further enhanced when I sat in Peter Close's development circle (a weekly seance in which a medium teaches a small group of people how to communicate with the spirit). They are now very close to me, often guiding me during times of difficulty, and they advise me of the appropriate words to say to my sitters. Without the protection and wisdom of these spiritual helpers a medium's work would be fraught with danger.

For many years I worked as a professional artist and, as I put paint to canvas, I would become so immersed in my work that I would enter a different state of consciousness – an inspired state of creative revelry. Artists often refer to this as being inspired by the Muse, but when the Muse started to talk to me I began to wonder whether there was a conscious being behind the voice. At first the inner voice would guide my artistic activities but gradually it started to give me advice about my life. When I followed the instructions it invariably proved to be the right advice which took into account situations that I was unaware of at the time.

Perhaps the voice was my own inner voice? Could I prove otherwise? The voice always gave helpful, encouraging advice but was it healthy to encourage it? I had met a number of schizophrenics and saw at close hand how uncontrolled voices could torment their soul.

The answers to my questions came suddenly and with such force that I could no longer dodge the issue. It was as if the ground fell from underneath me and I was floating in a black void. Before me was a light so beautiful that I instinctively fell towards it. As I did so I felt my personality being stripped away. Everything I cherished and held dear fell away from me. I knew that what was happening was an irreversible process. If I went with the experience I would never be the same again. I might even no longer exist.

A voice called to me across the void. 'Let go! Let go!' Every possible excuse to resist flooded my mind. With every excuse came the same answer. 'Let go! Let go!' I stopped resisting and did as instructed. I let go of everything that was me and tumbled towards the light. I dissolved into infinity.

It is impossible to explain in words the experience that followed. To say that I became infinite light is not enough, for light is of the world. To say that I went beyond form is not enough, for I was beyond form, yet one with it. To say that I became one with God is not enough, for the word God has too many associations and limited preconceptions.

I emerged into a joyful abstract world that had form but not as we understand it in our dimension. Beside me stood a young Buddhist Tibetan monk. 'When everything dissolves, all that is left is love,' he said. He was expressing the words that I found impossible to formulate. 'Are you real?' I asked, 'or are you my higher self?' He smiled. 'I cannot answer that question. The experience you have just had was real, was it not? Does it matter if I am real or not? Judge me only by the truth that I speak. If I cease to speak truth, then please reject me.' A life-long friendship had begun.

Over the years I have now accepted that the monk, who gives the name Taratha, is real. He has spoken through me in trance and given messages that other mediums have confirmed. Occasionally other mediums have even repeated the exact words of instruction that he has spoken to me the previous day. He has told me facts about Tibet that I have been able to check in obscure Tibetan texts and says that one day he will be able to confirm his identity beyond question. I will just have to wait and see, but as he himself said, does it really matter? All that matters is the truth of his words.

Taratha is not my only spirit helper. There are others too, and many of these are not on a high plane of spiritual understanding. For example, an Italian clown, who works with me during my public demonstrations, has to be held in check by the other guides. He shows me how to make the audience laugh and so raise the vibrations to make spirit communication easier. His favourite trick is to press the spirit communicators for stories and anecdotes about false teeth. It was him who brought forward the story about the lady who carried her father's false teeth to the funeral (see p.92) and other stories of glorious grandmothers who edged their pies with them. I could write a book about stories of false teeth given as proof of the afterlife!

Each one of my guides has given me subjective and objective proof of their reality. I call them the wingless angels. At my circle that meets every Wednesday evening and has been featured on the television documentary *The Magic and Mystery Show* (see p.33), Taratha talks to the group. I enter a trance that deepens as Taratha takes control. At first I am vaguely conscious of what is being said, but within a few moments I lose nearly all awareness of the discourse given. I enter what I can only describe as a light-headed awareness. I am surrounded by a peaceful inner light and hear my voice speaking far away. Like a faint, overheard conversation across a crowded room the words are heard but unintelligible to me.

My regular sitters include intelligent people who are not predisposed to fantasy. The reality of the trance is further confirmed when, if the power is high and the trance deep, the guides will allow someone known to one of the sitters to communicate directly through me. They have been able to provide evidence of survival and the spirit communicator is recognized by their voice, gesture and the nature of the private information given to the sitters at the seance.

I will now recount one of these sessions that was recorded on cassette during a period of trance. I was completely unconscious of what was being said during this spirit communication.

A message from a wingless angel

Good evening, my friends. The talks I have given you in our discourses so far have all addressed the same fundamental question: What is the nature of reality? My answer is simple. There is only one reality. And that reality is God. You may call Him by a different name – the absolute, Brahman, Allah, infinite consciousness, omnipresent love, limitless energy, the cosmic sea of being, Nirvana – but in the end it is all the same. God is One. It is the same God that inspires every religion.

God is both personal and infinite. He is manifest and unmanifest. He is conscious and unconscious. He has form and no form. As you talk to me you can also talk to God in your heart. As I answer your questions so God too can answer your questions when you look within. For you are a manifestation of God but you are separated from this realization by ignorance. Matter and the world of spirit are nothing other than the concrete thoughts of God. The quest of life on earth and of life in the Spirit is to realize your oneness with God, to remove the veils of ignorance.

Like sunlight that shines through a stained-glass window, the one reality has separated into many forms. You see only the spectrum of the world before your eyes but there exist worlds within worlds. I talk to you from one of these worlds that lies beyond material form. I talk to you from beyond the threshold of what you erroneously call death.

Your world and the Spirit World are One. It is too easy to think of the spirit world as being separate from your own. But it is not, the two worlds are of the same reality but you are not fully aware of this truth. The same fundamental energy vibrates at different frequencies to create different worlds. The universe of matter is only one part of this spectrum of vibration. In time science will understand this. The world of form is a sluggish vibration where matter can only be manipulated with matter. In the Spirit and the higher planes the substance of our world is manipulated by mind alone. The constant throughout Creation is not material light but the 'light' of consciousness. Awareness exists on all planes of being.

So, you will understand, energy takes different forms depending on how it vibrates and many parallel worlds are thereby created. The spirit world, like the world of matter, has form but is more malleable and can be changed and manipulated by mind. Consequently, when a person first enters the Spirit they see a world that is familiar to them; a beautified version of the world they knew on earth. But soon they discover that the Spirit does not have as many limitations as earthly life. Time here does not travel in a straight line, communication is made directly between minds, travel takes place at the speed of thought and perfect worlds are created by mind and limited only by the imagination.

A spiritually advanced soul will quickly see that there are few limitations yet those who bring with them their earthly desires will continue to live in an earth-like reality. For many, the afterlife is intrinsically the same as on earth: they eat, sleep, live in houses and continue the routines they once knew. But the soul that is inspired by spiritual love will continue to progress. They will see that the work on themselves must continue – even in heaven. Beyond the spirit planes are higher planes still, planes that they must ultimately progress to. Their heart's desire will be to progress onward, to be liberated from form and personality, ultimately to merge with the Godhead. Inner prompting and guidance from advanced souls will reveal to them that their goal is to return to the source and become angelic beings. Self-realization comes when the soul no longer clings, when it lets go, when it falls in love with the divine. For love is giving; love is surrender.

In life you have free will, but once union with the Godhead has been realized your will and God's will become one.

The spiritual quest that I have outlined is emerging today in the hearts of many seekers. The religions of the world can no longer quench the thirst for spiritual truth. Where once words and belief were enough, today the seekers want to know and experience the truth for themselves. You will witness, in the coming years, the bankruptcy and near collapse of religion. As this happens you will also see many environmental, economic and political troubles in your world. But as the old form dies a new light emerges that will illuminate the ancient religious teachings and strip away the self-righteous arrogance that has prohibited direct contact with God.

Where once there was fanaticism and separatism, now there will be modesty and unity.

To bring this change about, many angelic beings from our world have incarnated in human form. They come to reawaken the ancient knowledge that has for so long been lost or distorted. You will see miracles. The bigoted will lose their power and stranglehold on truth as seekers realize for themselves the true reality. From India, Russia, Brazil, Japan, America and Europe the universal religion will be born to transform the world. But it will not be as the religions you once knew. The new religion will be enthroned in the heart. It shall have no form or doctrine yet will animate every religion. It shall not be founded on fear but will express itself as love.

Chapter Nine
Reincarnation

Reincarnation is one of the world's oldest beliefs that dates back to the times of the ancient Greeks and early Indian civilizations. Many people today, from all walks of life, believe that they have lived before. Included in this chapter are the stories of some ordinary people with astonishing memories of lives from long ago.

Do you believe that you have lived before? Have you had a recurring dream set in another time and place, or do you have a nagging feeling that you were once someone else? Reincarnation was once a taboo subject, but in today's tolerant society many people are coming forward to say they are convinced that they have lived before. The previous lives they describe are not necessarily about being a person of great importance. Most talk about the tedium of previous ages and often believe themselves to have been thoroughly dislikeable characters.

Belief in reincarnation is common in the East, particularly among Hindus and Buddhists, but much rarer in Western culture. However, the concept is not entirely alien to us. The ancient Greeks, particularly Orpheus, Pythagoras and Plato, talked of the migration of the soul through different lives, both human and animal. The early Christian Church also accepted the principle, which was expounded by Gnostics and by numerous Church fathers, including Clement of Alexandria, Origen and Saint Jerome. The doctrine was only declared a heresy 553 years after the death of Christ by the Second Council of Constantinople.

In modern times there has been a great deal of research into the claims of people who say they have remembered their previous lives. One of the best-known cases concerns Shanti Devi, born in Delhi in 1926. At the age of seven she told her mother that she had been alive before, in a town called Muttra. Over the next two years her recall of events increased until she was telling her parents about her previous husband, their house, and their three children. At the age of nine a complete stranger came to the door to discuss business with her father and Shanti claimed she recognized him as her husband's cousin from her previous life.

To the astonishment of everyone the man did live in Muttra and agreed that his cousin's wife, Ludgi, had died ten years earlier. When the husband came to visit her, Shanti recognized him immediately and flung herself into his arms. When she was taken to Muttra, she was able to direct the carriage to Ludgi's house and identified her father-in-law sitting in front of it. She also recognized her two eldest children, but not the youngest, whose birth had cost Ludgi her life.

Past-life therapy

There is now a growing wealth of cases like Shanti's that are sugges-tive of reincarnation and today many people are exploring ways to unlock their own lost memories. Some people have spontaneous recall but there are also professionals who will help you unlock your hidden memories. Most past-life therapists use deep relaxation sessions or hypnotic techniques to guide their clients back into time. Firstly they encourage them to recall events in this life and then back into early childhood. A point comes when they can ask the subject to now look to the time before their birth and describe what they see and feel. Some describe a period between lives where they live in a heavenly afterlife but most jump straight to memories of other lives from history.

Of course, this is fascinating psychological experimentation, but it is also claimed that regression into past lives has a therapeutic effect. There are many cases on record to indicate that the illnesses we expe-rience in this life are the traces left by the traumatic experiences brought forwards from past lives. For example, a person suffering from severe eczema may discover that in a past life they were burnt to death. By reliving the experience they understand the root cause of their physical problems and the blemishes disappear after the therapy session. There are many cases on record where psychological prob-lems and physical illness have been healed after a period of past-life therapy.

In the East reincarnation is seen as the progression of the soul through many lives on earth, as through grades in a school, before it 'graduates' to the immortal perfection of oneness with the infinite. Throughout this progress we accumulate *karma*, which is a Sanskrit word taken from the word *karoti* meaning 'he does', and is used to describe the effects of past actions. The Western equivalent would be Christ's maxim 'as you sow, so shall you reap'. In Hinduism a person's karma follows him or her from incarnation to incarnation until fulfilled or spiritually transcended.

Of course, all these 'memories' of past lives may be fantasy, or they could be genetic memories, or even clairvoyance of the past. The brain is an incredible storehouse of unconscious memory and in a hypnotic trance can be coaxed to recall vast amounts of information. A page from a book glanced at in childhood can be recalled word for word by a hypnotized adult many years later. The miraculous cures could be psychosomatic and recalling past lives may just be a way of resolving psychological problems through fantasy. The evidence for reincarnation will always be a subject for debate, but the fact is that more people than ever before are coming forward to claim that they have lived previously.

Case File 1

'The other woman' in Richard King's marriage is literally out-of-this-world. Richard believes that he and his friends are in communication with his soul mate, Lorelei, with whom he has shared many past lives. According to Richard his wife doesn't mind:

> At first she was upset that I gave my attention to someone else but gradually she's coming around. After all Lorelei is not here in the physical sense and I've obviously chosen to live this life with my wife Jo.

For six years Richard has been writing a 'spiritual CV' about his past lives at the astonishing rate of 80,000 words a year. Most of this concerns the lives he has shared with his soul mate Lorelei.

> My interest started in 1991 when I took part in a healing workshop at the Healing Arts Festival in London. We did some relaxation exercises and were then asked to visualize our spirit guides. At first I saw nothing, then suddenly, I saw a woman's face in full colour and vivid detail. I felt that I knew her, and that we had been deeply, physically, in love many times. It was an intense, all pervading love of such quality, depth, beauty and sheer power – beautiful beyond words and utterly devastating. It left me shattered and in tears.

It was a psychic friend, Leigh, who first referred to Richard's new friend as a soul mate:

Over the following months I came to understand the term better and realized that there was vastly more to it than the usual concept of soul mates. One Sunday evening as I sat thinking about the emotional side of my nature I heard a voice say, 'That's connected with a previous life. Lorelei has already told you that.' Over the next few days an extraordinary series of coincidences, involving myself, friends and family, reinforced the connection between my soul mate and the name Lorelei.

One evening after attending a healing session, Leigh and I were in a coffee shop. Leigh said he was seeing mountains connected with me and asked if I had been to Italy or Austria. I said that a healer had just made a similar connection.

Then Leigh said of my soul mate Lorelei, 'She's not just anyone, she's the one to do with the legend.' Leigh asked if there was a connection somewhere with the Black Forest in Germany and the Rhine. He saw us together playing on rocks and swimming in a large river.

When Richard and Leigh searched their history books they discovered that there was a mythical woman called Lorelei. The French poet Apollinaire had written about her as goddess in the poem 'Bacharach', describing her as a woman, 'Who made all men perish from love'. According to the legends she lived near the Black Forest at the famous crag that overhangs the Rhine downstream from Bacharach in Germany. For Richard King, Lorelei is a real person with whom he has shared past lives:

During development circles and at other times, I began to see parts of other lives, my own and, occasionally, other people's. Lives I had spent with Lorelei included one during the English Civil War. In those days she was known as Marjorie. I was called Jeremy and our children were Ann-Marie and Toby.

Some people joke that having Lorelei around is like being haunted by the ghost of an ex-wife. It is not like that. Lorelei is a powerful healing spirit. In mediumistic communications she calls my wife Jo her Celestial Sister. This was proved to Jo and I when Jo had to have a hysterectomy. I sat in meditation asking Lorelei to send healing to her as the operation took place. I saw Jo and Lorelei surrounded in a pink cloud of healing light. The doctors were amazed at Jo's remarkable recovery and she was home within just a few days of the operation.

Richard King's experience may be psychological. Lorelei may be his anima – the female side of his psyche. However, there are details in this story that suggest otherwise.

Rosemary Barry started having waking dreams at the age of 13, which recurred for six years:

> It was like dreaming while you're wide awake. All of a sudden I would be transported back in time to Victorian times. I find myself standing by a bandstand and notice the distinctive circular patterns of the iron work. I am wearing a long dress with a small floral pattern; I have gloves on and am wearing a bonnet. At my side is a man in a military uniform. He has a sword and his tunic reminds me of the uniforms from the times of the Crimean War.

In 1970 at the age of 19 Rosemary courted a young man called Michael:

> While in London Michael suggested that we take a walk in Richmond Park. I was overcome by an eerie feeling of *déjà vu* as we walked down the paths. Although I'd never been there before I realized that I knew every detail of the place. I took Michael's hand and to his astonishment was able to show him around the park. I could tell him where the paths led and what we'd see when we turned each bend. I felt as if I was living in two worlds at the same time.
>
> Then the eerie feeling got worse. My head was in a spin and I felt as if I was falling through space into an empty void. This was the place of my dreams, but now it was real. For a few moments I was standing in another time. I could see my floral dress, feel my bonnet and could see Michael beside me in full military uniform. We walked on and turned a corner. There in front of us was the bandstand with the same distinctive wrought ironwork!

Rosemary explained to Michael why she had been behaving so strangely and began to tell him of her vision:

> Michael wouldn't let me finish. He confessed that he too had persistent dreams of what he believed was a past life. He had been a soldier who had died at the 'Charge of the Light Brigade' during the Crimean War!

Although it appears that Rosemary and Michael had shared a past life together, their relationship in this life was to end:

> I believe that we had to come together to resolve unfinished business. We parted in sorrow at that bandstand all those years ago, but were given a second chance to resolve our relationship.

The experience of recalling a past life inspired Rosemary to become a past-life therapist and she now helps others recall their incarnations. She teaches people to get into a state of light revelry similar to the waking dreams she described earlier. One of her subjects is her daughter Victoria, who describes the following experience:

> I was quite a tomboy at the age of 13 when Mum offered to take me back to my past life. It was more than a phase. I loved war films and had a thing about helicopters.
>
> When Mum guided me back I became aware that I was in Vietnam. I was an American soldier aged 21. I was a man but I was still me, it felt quite natural being male. Five of us were parachuted into the jungle but one of us was captured and we saw him executed by the Vietcong. We became angry and started shooting at the enemy even though we were greatly outnumbered. Then there was a frantic chase through the jungle as we dashed to catch the helicopters that had been sent in to pick us up. To my horror I saw one of the helicopters hit and explode. In desperation I rushed towards the second helicopter but was shot in the back and died before I could reach it.

Rosemary says that during her recall Victoria was crying out in anger and pain. She wept as she described events as if they were happening here and now. This leads Rosemary to comment:

> There are people who may say that past-life recall is a fantasy. But the subject is doing much more than story-telling. They live the events and express an intensity of emotion that is totally unfamiliar to them. These impressions and feelings have to come from somewhere. I believe it is from past lives.

Case File 3

Ian Cugley was apprehensive when he decided in October 1997 to be hypnotized by past-life therapist Diane Egby-Edwards. Ian is a down-to-earth man who spent much of his working life managing the staff of British Steel's stores. Using hypnotism Diane was able to take Ian back to his previous life:

I'd always felt that it's mainly sad old people looking for comfort who want to know what lies before and after this life. But I put aside my scepticism and decided to give hypnotic regression a go. To my utter surprise it answered many questions about why things are the way they are in my life.

Although I've never travelled and I've never read history I have an uncanny ability to recall America's early history. I've never been taught it but I just *know* it. It was this era that I found myself in when Diana took me back.

I found myself stood looking across a very broad valley with red rock mountains in the distance. It was hot and I was being harassed by flies and I was very, very thirsty. I was wearing cavalry trousers with buckskin knee boots. I saw three ladies carrying parasols and looking at me with great suspicion.

I walked across a street and went into a bar. As I came out I realized that I was still so very thirsty. Diane then asked me to move forward in time and I found myself on a horse travelling over some very arid land and came to some trees where there were some cavalry camped. As I approached I could sense the bad feelings coming from them. In the distance I could hear Diane's voice asking me if I'm a deserter. 'No, I'm not,' I replied. 'I don't know what I am, but they don't like me.'

I spoke to the officer in charge and complained about my thirst. I was then brought forward by Diane and found myself walking across a plain looking for a wagon that was overdue. It was desperate that we found it. I then saw that it was being chased by native Americans. I said 'What am I to do?' At this point Diana told me to look at my hands. 'Oh,' I exclaimed 'I'm brown! I'm a native American!'

It was such a shock to me at the time and perhaps explained why nobody had given me water. I then chased after the wagon, hoping that they would realize that I wasn't hostile, but I got trapped beneath it when it rolled over. Pinned beneath the wagon I experienced the horror of seeing the native Americans fire flaming arrows and I was burnt to death.

The experience was so vivid, so real, that I now believe it to be memories of a past life. It also explains a lot about my own life. As a child I would be the only one in the cinema who would cheer on the native Americans. Many years ago I started collecting plates portraying native Americans, dream-catchers and mandalas, and I'd always felt that the native Americans are misrepresented by history. This all started way before it became fashionable to talk about native Americans.

Discovering my past life was a strange but wonderful experience. I am no longer a sceptic.

(Case File 4)

Jannet Stone added the unusual extra 'n' to her Christian name soon after her divorce, although she wasn't sure about her reasons for doing this:

> I don't know why but I felt absolutely compelled to do it. At the time I thought it was something to do with finding a new identity but I was soon to discover that the reason for my action is be found far in the past.

Jannet, like many people after a divorce, started a spiritual search to find her real self. She met hypnotherapist Rosemary Barry who helped her explore her past lives by means of regression psychometry. This is a psychic technique that does not involve hypnotism or trance. The psychometrist intuitively senses their clients' past lives by holding an object that the person has owned for a long time and reading the 'recordings' left on it. Jannet goes on:

> I was fascinated to hear about my past lives. I was told that I once lived in Delft in Holland during the latter part of the seventeenth century. We were a merchant family and lived under a cloud of religious intolerance. A man was important who sailed the barges. He had given me a ring.
>
> Of course, there was no way we could know for sure that Rosemary was getting it right. Then she looked at me and said, 'I see something very important that you will be able to confirm one day. The ring has a coat of arms on it. I think it's a puffin bird, no, it's a helmet seen from the side.' She then drew the picture that she was seeing. 'You'll find this in Delft, there's flowing feathers and there's a funny cross man or something above it.'

At this time Jannet was a mature student studying history of art:

> Only weeks after the consultation I was given the opportunity to go to Holland to study the paintings of Vermeer. Of course, as soon as I had some free time I shot down to Delft to visit the local church and see if I could find my coat of arms.

Jannet visited St Hypolitus, Delft's old sixteenth-century church, but was disappointed to discover that the graves had been vandalized by French invaders in 1789. All the crests and coats of arms had been hacked off. But as she turned to leave something caught her eye:

> I noticed one grave by the door that had a coat of arms. My hair felt like it was curling as I saw the helmet shaped like a puffin's head, the flowing feathers and even the strange cross figure that Rosemary had tried to describe. Then I looked at the inscription and nearly fell backwards. The name of one of the grave's occupants spelt her name the same way as me – Jannetgen.

Case File 5

Amanda McCallum had always wanted to try hypnotic regression. When she saw hypnotist Kevin Taylor's advertisement in her local newsagent's shop window she decided to give it a try. What she uncovered was to amaze her and change her life:

> During our first session I saw myself as a male sailor in the eighteenth century. It was an incredible experience. I felt like a man and cursed like a man and could see scenes of eighteenth-century Portsmouth unfolding before my eyes. I was shocked by the incredible sharpness and vividness of the experience. This was not dream or suggestion. It was as if I was really there.
>
> Kevin, the hypnotist, was also amazed at how easily I entered deep trance. I was such a good subject that he asked me if I would mind coming back and doing some research to see just how much we could uncover. Normally I'm so shy that I'd have said no, but I liked Kevin and felt I could trust him. I agreed to help.
>
> Kevin and I seemed to get on with each other from the moment we met. It's quite unlike me to trust someone so implicitly, but with Kevin it was as if I'd known him all my life. We continued the sessions and I remembered a number of past lives. We got on so very well that finally Kevin asked me the big question. Next time he hypnotized me, could he ask me to recall if we had ever shared a past life together?
>
> Kevin fired the question at the next hypnotic session. I became this young woman of 18 who spoke with a tremendous self-confidence and assertiveness that was nothing like my real personality. 'I am Melissa,' I heard my voice boom, 'and why are you asking me such foolish questions that you know already?'

Melissa spoke in an Old English dialect and used words such as 'hexed' which I wouldn't use in ordinary speech. When my Mum listened to the tape she said that it certainly was my voice but definitely not my personality.

Melissa told Kevin that we were in Cornwall, it was the sixteenth century and that she was a witch. She called Kevin 'David' and said that he was one of her companions. There were other companions, such as a man called Simeon, but David was her favourite. David would help Melissa to gather herbs, bless babies and conduct healing rituals. I saw my past life unfold. I saw us dancing naked in water under the moonlight, riding bareback horses along the beach and saw how David had helped me raise a child in the same way my mother had raised me to be a witch. I died at the age of 47 which I described as 'a ripe old age to die'. But what amazed me most was just how different a person I was. I was cocky, authoritarian and sometimes downright vulgar.

When I came around and woke to my normal self my cheeks flushed with embarrassment. I had known Kevin for only a month and here I was talking about dancing naked with him in the moonlight. You don't normally tell a stranger this type of thing.

I believe that the hypnotic sessions have rekindled a romance from long ago. I'm nothing like Melissa in this life, I'm just an ordinary, down-to-earth mother of two. If someone had told me this same story a year ago I'd have thought them completely mad. But Kevin and I really do now believe that we lived together once before, hundreds of years ago. We've talked about visiting another hypnotist to have Kevin hypnotized. I can't wait to hear what David really thought about his mentor Melissa.

Case File 6

Josephine Sellers recalls the day she met her future husband Brian:

We were meant for each other and we knew it the moment our eyes met. I felt as if an electric charge shot through my body when I spotted Brian towering over the group of men with him. I married him at 19 and we've been together ever since.

I believe that it was no coincidence that we met and fell in love. Our coming together was predetermined because we had been together before, 400 years ago. As a child I used to have memories of living in a big house and riding in a carriage. I would ask my mother where all the people were that I once knew, the 'yesterday people' as I called them. 'And who's the vicar?' I would say to my friends. Of course, Mother told me that this was all nonsense and I became as sceptical as her and about the existence of past lives. But in time my mother changed her mind.

In the early years of our marriage we lived in London and I had a busy life working as a legal assistant. Life was so hectic that there was hardly time to think, but when I stopped work and started a family something strange started to happen to me. Some mornings I would wake up and find myself in the wrong time. I'd sit up in bed and realize that I was in a luxurious Elizabethan room. I was watching events that took place hundreds of years ago. It was like watching a film, except you could feel and smell everything as well. These visions would end as abruptly as they began.

My visions triggered my interest in the paranormal and I started to meet many people who were psychic. So many of them said the same thing to me: I would live in a cottage that would have a very special significance for me. This was a very odd thing to say to someone living in the London suburbs.

One year we went to Dorset for our holidays and I just didn't want to go back home to London. I became very upset and started crying and Brian felt the same. We decided there and then that we'd close our business in London and move as soon as we could. The pull of Dorset was like a magnet.

We finally moved and settled in a small cottage in Wimborne. The psychics' prophecies had come true.

I felt that something had happened there in the past that I now wanted to put right. In particular I was drawn to an area called Witchampton and would go there at every opportunity.

Brian and I started to take an interest in psychic things and after ten years' experimentation we eventually met a trance medium named Evelyn who took no fee for her work. Spirit voices would talk directly through her. Then one day, to my utter astonishment, a vicar started to talk through her. 'My name is Reverend William Thomas,' he said, 'and I am here to tell you a remarkable tale of reincarnation.' Over a number of sessions he told us that he was the man I had seen in my childhood. He also told me how he'd had many legal battles with the crown over tenure rights. But most intriguing of all was that he said that we knew each other. I had been a woman called Catherine and had known him 400 years ago during the Elizabethan times.

I immediately realized that I was being told things that I somehow already knew. I recorded each session and to make sure everything was authenticated correctly asked a sceptical ex-army major and ex-school master, Mr John Lloyd, to help research any information I was given. We continued our sessions with the medium and spoke again to the Rev. William Thomas. We also made tape recordings and locked the tapes away in a bank vault. Later I met a hypnotist, Diane Egby-Edwards, who offered to hypnotize me and take me back to my past life to see if we could retrieve any more information. I also kept careful notes of any memories that would come to me spontaneously.

At first, I really couldn't believe what was happening. But the combined information given us from my hypnosis session, from the medium and from my own spontaneous memories gave us enough information to search the records to see if it was all true. I was told that I was named Catherine. I was the middle daughter of five from a family of 13 children. One of my brother's names was Edmund. The vicar also gave us detailed information about his legal battles with the crown.

But there was more to come. In the trance sessions the vicar told us that we had all shared this past life together. The researcher Lloyd had been the father, Sir Henry, whom, incidentally the vicar despised, and my husband had been my brother Sir Edmund. According to the vicar we had all been together in this past life 400 years ago.

We went to the Dorset Records Office and looked to see if we could find any reverends with the name William Thomas. To our utter astonishment there was a vicar with this name for the small parish church of Chritchel, later named Witchampton – the place that had obsessed me so much since we'd moved. Also we found that he was connected with a landed family called Uvedale. The father was Sir Henry Uvedale, the mother Isabell and there were thirteen children including a Catherine and Edmund. Clearly this was the family that the vicar had talked about. Also, we discovered that the vicar had, as he had told us, been my tutor and involved in a long legal dispute with the crown. Everything we had been told was true.

We also discovered that the estate still existed although the original house had burned down. It was now owned by Mary Martin, who is a cousin of the present Queen. We contacted her ladyship, told her our strange story and asked if we could take a look around the grounds to see if it revealed any more memories. She gave us permission and invited us for tea.

I had remembered the big house, but couldn't remember living in it. With our group was a dowser, Bob Seethon, who said he would dowse the grounds to see if there were any other buildings below the ground. He found something and suddenly the memories came flooding back.

Brian and I, when we were Catherine and Edmund, hadn't lived in the big house at all. The thirteen children were such a handful that Sir Henry had build a separate nursery a quarter of a mile away from the house where we had been born. Together with the dowser we found the site.

Afterwards we asked Mary Martin if she knew if another building had stood in the grounds. Her ladyship said that her family had the original records and she believed that this was true.

I believe that these strange events prove that Brian and I have shared a past life before. But according to the spirit of Rev. William Thomas this is not our first life together. He says we also lived in the same area in 3000 BC when I was a pagan seer who carried a jewelled wand and worshipped at the ancient standing stones. The evidence for our Elizabethan life together is so overwhelming that I'm prepared to take the vicar on his word.

Chapter Ten

Miracles

I first heard the name of Sathya Sai Baba in 1973 when I was saving the money to travel overland to India with my friend Terry. 'You must visit his *ashram* (a religious retreat of Hindu holy men) while you're in India,' urged a fellow traveller. 'Incredible things are happening there.' Unfortunately I couldn't raise the money and abandoned my yearned-for trip. I never spoke or heard the name again until soon after I met Jane in 1988 when her friend, Jim Chivers (see p.21), gave us some light-grey ash (*vibhuti*) and suggested that we eat a little. He told us that the ash was considered holy by the Hindus and had been materialized by a Hindu avatar named Sathya Sai Baba. It was soon after this that the dreams started to happen.

I had seen a photo of Sathya Sai Baba but knew nothing of his philosophy or the story of his remarkable life and miracles. The photo I saw was of a little man wearing a brilliant orange robe and with a mop of black curly hair, a bit like Jimi Hendrix. At the time of writing he is 72 years of age, but in the photo I first saw he would have been about 45. I couldn't understand why I should start dreaming about him and why the dreams should be so remarkably vivid. These were the most amazingly lucid dreams that I had ever experienced.

My first dream was set in a garage where many cars were being fixed. Clad in his bright saffron orange robes, Sai Baba introduced himself as the chief mechanic and suggested that I come into his workshop and perhaps help a little, too. He showed me how to repair car engines. The dream made no sense.

A few weeks later Jane and I were invited to Jim Chiver's retirement party and there we met a number of his Indian friends who were devotees of Sai Baba. I was introduced to Babu, an elderly Indian man whose eyes sparkled and voice trembled when he spoke about his guru. I told him about the dream. 'It is a tremendous blessing to have a dream about Swami,' he said. 'Swami is calling you. He often tells his followers that he is like a mechanic of the soul and will call those that need his guidance into his workshop. When Swami comes to you in a dream it is not like a dream. It is real.'

Babu told me how a few years ago he was completely paralysed. The doctors had said that his condition was incurable and that he would remain like this for the rest of his life. He would never walk again. Babu prayed to his guru day and night. 'Then one night I saw an orange shimmer in my room,' says Babu. 'I looked again and was overjoyed to see Sai Baba appear in my room as real as you are now, sitting before me.'

That night the spiritual form touched Babu's feet and by the morning he could move his feet and toes. The next evening he saw Sai Baba again and the vision touched his waist. By the morning he could sit up unaided. On the third night Sai Baba touched Babu on the head and he could walk unaided. The doctors were amazed at Babu's spontaneous remission. Everyone I spoke to confirmed that he had been paralysed and had recovered. And perhaps the greatest testimony to truth was the great tears that rolled down this man's face as he told his story. I was certain that Babu was telling the truth.

Although I had read very little about Sai Baba, the dreams kept happening and Jane started having dreams too. 'I saw Sai Baba dressed in blue,' Jane told me. 'He asked me to sit beside him and added that I was to begin spiritual healing.' He came to us both in our dreams many times and we were each shown remarkable things and given spiritual instruction that greatly helped us with our mediumistic work. I decided to find out more about Sai Baba.

Sathya Sai Baba: a brief biography

Sathya Sai Baba was born in Puttaparthi, a remote village in southern India, on 23 November 1926. His parents named the baby Sathyanarayana Raju of the Kshatriya caste. The villagers tell of signs occurring shortly before his birth, such as musical instruments playing by themselves and soon after his birth a deadly cobra snake was found in his crib. Remarkably it had not harmed the baby. This event, and many others, were taken as auguries that a very special person had been born. The cobra is the symbol of Shiva, one of the three important divinities of the Hindu pantheon.

One version of the story goes that at the age of 13 the young Sathya was bitten by a scorpion and fell into a coma that lasted 24 hours. When he awoke he started quoting long passages of Sanskrit poetry and philosophy that were far beyond the scope of his limited schooling. His frightened parents took him to an exorcist, who shaved his head and cut multiple deep crosses into his skull, bidding the

> There is no need for me to command invisible spirits since my own divine will materializes the objects. I am everything, everywhere, omniscient, omnipotent and omnipresent; and so whatever I will, instantly happens. Like the qualities of truth, love and peace, these are things that generate the Atomic or Cosmic forces behind the universe.

As a child he had announced that until the age of 16 he would be mostly engaged in sportive pursuits, and that from then on, until the age of 32, he would be drawing people to him by means of *mahimas* ('miracles'). He said that without this display of power, 'no one can gauge even a fraction of my glory'.

Modern-day miracles

Many well-respected authors have investigated the miracles of Sai Baba for decades. There is not enough space here to cover their stories, and I do not want to repeat information that you can read elsewhere in detail. To find out more, I suggest you read any of the books by the following authors: Howard Murphet, Dr John Hislop, Dr Samuel Sandweiss or the catholic priest Don Mario Mazzoleni.

Some of the reports that you will read about Sai Baba's miracles are mind-boggling. He has supposedly raised the dead, multiplied food as Christ did with the bread and fishes, materialized valuable objects out of the air and turned water into petrol when a car ran out of fuel. There are stories of him materializing sweets directly into people's mouths, appearing in two or more places at the same time and projecting a photograph of Christ on to the film in someone's camera. His devotees have witnessed paranormal and psychic phenomena for which no common-sense explanation is possible. With a wave of his hand he can materialize sweets, images, idols, flowers, fruits, rosaries and crucifixes. So numerous, so well-attested and so extraordinary are these accounts that even the most die-hard sceptics find these 'miracles' hard to explain away.

Jane and I kept having the dreams about Sai Baba. Eventually I felt compelled to write about him in my books and newspaper columns. I started to receive some very interesting telephone calls and letters. Although I did not consider myself a devotee, I nonetheless had a great respect for the wisdom of his teachings. He claims to be omnipresent, so if this really is the case, I argued to myself, then he would be able to give me an answer as to whether I should write about him or not.

When starting an article, I closed my eyes and randomly opened a pile of papers about him that had been given me to me by a friend, Johnny Diamond, who had downloaded and printed them off from the Internet. I struck the page with a pin and read a quote from him: 'It is time the world knew.' I then picked up the phone to interview Joan Brake, who had written to my column. 'It's all right to talk about Sai Baba now you know,' said Joan. 'He says, "it is time the world knew".'

So it was with the hairs standing on the back of my neck that I began the interview with Joan, who, along with her husband Richard, had first heard about the miracles and teaching of Sai Baba over 11 years ago. Their search for spiritual truth had begun within Spiritualism. 'We found that, without a shadow of a doubt, life goes on after death', said Joan.

As Joan and Richard's search continued, they had looked into clairvoyance, meditation, reflexology, crystal therapy and native American teachings. 'If anything came along with a spiritual aspect, Richard and I would look into it and share what we found with others.' Inevitably, perhaps, Joan and Richard opened their home and, once a month, invited experts and lecturers to talk to their growing group:

> One by one they started to talk about Sai Baba, even though it was not the subject they'd come to talk about. I listened to the talks and saw videos of Sai Baba performing miracles, and although it was plain that he was a wonderful man, he was not doing or saying anything different to what Christ said. This type of thing has to be real for me. I can't accept everything people say is true.

But Richard and Joan became more and more intrigued:

> The people who spoke or wrote about Sai Baba weren't 'wild' or 'hippie' types. They were professional people, such as doctors, so we decided that if Christ was alive today then we'd want to go and see him. And if, from what I'd read and heard, Sai Baba was doing the same things as Christ, then we would have to go and find out for ourselves.

Joan and Richard joined a party of 90 people who had made the same decision, and flew to India. Nowadays Sai Baba is surrounded by so many followers that it is almost impossible to get near him. On his 70th birthday (23 November) he had over one million visitors to his *ashram*, yet every one of them was housed and fully fed for free. Joan and Richard were lucky. They were invited to meet Sai Baba for a private audience with him. Joan goes on:

> Years and years ago there was a song in the hit parade called, 'Open the Door Richard'. A family joke, that continued for years, was to change the words and sing, 'Close the Door Richard' every time Richard entered a room. Richard was the last to enter Sai Baba's private chambers. With a twinkle in his eye Sai Baba looked at him and in the correct tune actually sang the words 'Close the Door... Richard'! Sai Baba then turned round, looked at me, and roared with laughter.
>
> Nobody else in that room knew what was going on, but for Richard and me it was incredible that Sai Baba should know this little family joke from so long ago. It was absolutely fantastic.

Joan and Richard have since had a number of private interviews with Sai Baba over the years:

> On many occasions we've seen him materialize objects from thin air. On one occasion he materialized a silver medallion with his image imprinted on it, which was passed round. He then blew on it and it changed into a little golden statue of the Hindu elephant god, Ganesha, with three rubies hanging from it. This again was passed around. Sai Baba then looked at one of the visitors and said, 'What do you want?' 'You, Swami,' was the reply. So Sai Baba blew on it again and back came the medallion.
>
> I've seen him materialize rings with pictures of Christ on them, *vibhuti* ash, silver boxes, a whole list of things.

Joan stresses that the phenomena which Sai Baba displays are unimportant:

> When he looks at you, you know that he knows everything about you. I cannot explain the feeling of overwhelming love you feel in his presence. It's not hysterical. It's a silent, inward transformation.

I asked Joan what message this Eastern teacher can give to the West:

> His teachings are simply profound. Everyone can identify with what he says. It's like he's brought all the ancient wisdom up-to-date. Yet he's not trying to convert people, or make them change their faith. A Chris-

tian should remain a Christian, a Hindu a Hindu, etc. Perhaps it can best be expressed by quoting his words: 'There's only one religion: the religion of love. There's only one language: the language of the heart. There's only one caste: the caste of humanity. And there's only one God: and he is omnipresent.'

On the subject of Sai Baba, I have also received a number of interesting e-mails to my web site. This one from a doctor was very interesting:

I'm a medical doctor, 43 years old, with about twenty years' experience and now in a private practice. I came to know about Sathya Sai Baba about three years ago, and ever since have got stuck to him. It is beyond my comprehension to explain his miracles. I write to you with my first-hand experiences, to tell you about something that I've observed with my own eyes. One day I noticed liquid coming out of a picture of Sai Baba from outside the glass. It was pouring out from the side of his blessing palm, but only a little in quantity. It dripped down slowly. My wife is also a medical doctor. I've two daughters, one 7 years, one 9 years. There's no foul play. The question is: How can this liquid issue forth from the picture of Sai Baba, from the glass outside? In fact the neighbouring Lord Ganesha picture was 'sweating' similar *amrith* (a sweet nectar that tastes like honey), also all over the glass. How on earth can we explain this, that is the question. Since you expound the unexplainable, please explain this phenomenon.

The doctor had witnessed a phenomena that has been occurring in many homes throughout the world where *vibhuti* and its liquid equivalent, *amrith*, materializes on photographs of Sai Baba.

Jane, our eight-year-old daughter Danielle, and myself were to experience this first-hand. One of my readers telephoned me and asked if I'd like to visit a house in London where *vibhuti* ash was materializing all the time. I was told that it regularly appeared on photographs of Sai Baba. He could make an appointment for us to visit and witness this for ourselves.

The little house in Kingsbury, London, was nothing special to look at. It was a typical suburban house set in a nondescript area of the capital. It would have been hard to deliberately choose a more unremarkable setting for a miracle to happen.

We were greeted by Bhasker Joshi and his wife, Hema, who welcomed us into their home and led us into their living room. The whole house was filled with the subtle jasmine-scented perfume of the *vibhuti* ash which covered the many photographs that hung around the room. For a few moments we stood in silence looking at the surreal scene. Then Bhasker said:

> The writing, which is a little hard to read under the ash, says 'Love Swami'. It appeared by itself and the cross of *vibhuti* on this picture appeared on Good Friday. The photos were completely covered, but we removed the area around Swami's face. If we clear a section of the pictures the *vibhuti* reforms.

I was reminded of Sai Baba's words: 'My *shakti*, my power, my mystery can never be understood, whosoever may try, for however long a period, by whatever means.' Once we had time to absorb the wonderful atmosphere of this place, we sat down with Bhasker and Hema, and they told us their remarkable story. Bhasker began:

> I am of Brahmin caste, so was brought up in the ways of the Hindu religion. But nothing prepared me for the marvellous experiences I was to have on discovering Sai Baba when I was in Uganda in 1968. This was the only time Swami has left India, but I sat with about 2,000 people to catch sight of him. This is called *darshan* which means 'sight of the divine'. Sai Baba points his finger at me. 'Go inside,' my friend Dr Patel urged me. 'He wants to see you in the interview room!'
>
> Once I entered the room I touched Swami's feet, as is Hindu custom. Sai Baba smiled at me, then waved his hand and materialized a photograph of himself. I have a knack of losing things but this photograph has been upon my person every day since the interview. He knew everything about my life and told me how to resolve many personal problems which no one except myself and God knew about. To my wife, Hema, he turned and said, 'I am in this house.'
>
> At Sai Baba's 69th birthday celebrations in Harrow, London, we met Stephen Turoff who is a famous trance-healer and now a Sai Baba devotee. His entranced eyes looked at Hema. 'I will see you tonight,' he said. But it wasn't Stephen's voice; we all distinctly heard the soft tones of Sai Baba.

Hema excitedly took up the story:

> The next night I awoke in the middle of the night and saw Sai Baba standing in our bedroom! He walked towards me and I felt him touch

my forehead. 'Your problems are over, I am in your house now,' he said, then disappeared. In the morning we discovered that *vibhuti* had materialized in the prayer room, on the pictures of our Hindu deities and on photographs of Sai Baba.

Bhasker went on:

> The phenomena have continued ever since. And we are not the only people to experience these phenomena in our home. Nearby at Queensbury Mr Vadagama has been having *vibhuti* materialize in the machines at his factory. He tells us that one day he had an eight-ton machine to move over a bank holiday, but was let down at the last minute. If the machine wasn't moved immediately, he would lose a great deal of money as the tenant was to move in the next day. Like a good Hindu he prayed in his heart for help.
>
> A slim man in oily jeans walked into the warehouse. He had a lorry parked outside. 'You want to move the machine?' he said nonchalantly. Mr Vadagama asked the man if he could help and how much it would cost. He gave the man £75, which he counted slowly with his oily hands. Mr Vadagama turned his back for a few seconds to discover that the man had gone and to his utter bafflement saw that the eight-ton machine was all neatly dismantled and stacked on the truck.
>
> Two years later Mr Vadagama went to Puttaparthi and was seated among other devotees for *darshan*. Sai Baba walked up to him. 'Is your machine all right?' asked Swami with a broad smile across his face. 'You gave me £75 didn't you? I put it back in the machine. Go and check.' Immediately afterwards Mr Vadagama telephoned his daughter who was minding the business back in London. He told him where Sai Baba had said the money was and his daughter went to check. 'It's all there and has oily finger prints all over it,' came the excited reply.

Bhasker and Hema went on to tell me how the *vibhuti* ash will fill various sweet jars in the room upstairs that is set up as Sai Baba's own room. Also how *amrith* will pour from the pictures at auspicious times. Even food that is put before their temple is eaten. Credibility was beginning to strain. It could, of course, all be a well-meant hoax. Inwardly I asked Sai Baba for a tangible sign to prove that this was all true. Moments later a lady who had arrived at the same time as us opened the prayer letter that she had placed on the altar – to her astonishment the pages inside were covered in a light sprinkling of *vibhuti* ash.

Defining the undefinable

I had an interesting e-mail correspondence with Bon Giovanni, an American who has a web site dedicated to Sai Baba. He had read my articles on my web site, and wrote to me to correct a few names that I had misspelled. As Bon Giovanni clearly had personal experience of Sai Baba's miracles, I asked him to clear up a problem I had. Reading the many books about Swami, I had noticed that Sai Baba had contradicted himself. For example to one devotee he said that spiritual healing was good and to another that it was bad. He has also been asked if there is life on other planets and if there are really UFOs. Again he appears to offer us a contradiction, saying to some that they exist, and to others that they don't. Here is a small part of the explanation offered by Bon Giovanni:

> Swami had taken a group of students and two elders out to a forest reserve, where wild animals roamed, and all had sat down for tiffin, seated in a horseshoe with Baba at the centre of the group. A student, keen on such things, then asked Swami why he had told differing accounts to people about UFOs, since he really wanted to know if they were, or were not, real. Swami looked at the young man and started to answer, but at that moment in the field behind him, in broad daylight, a UFO appeared and just hovered there in the sky above the group. Not even looking back behind him, Baba calmly said, 'UFOs are just imagination', and the craft vanished.
>
> Since, as you say, that is important for you, then perhaps you want to find 'contradictions' in what Swami says. I suggest you examine very, very, very carefully why it bothers you, and see what happens. I truly no longer harbour such thoughts, and so cannot answer you. You see, Swami does extraordinary things. Sometimes he does such miracles that the mind simply caves in, and at other times he does such clumsy sleight-of-hand tricks that you think that he must think you are a fool if he expects you to fall for it. Why does he do that? Why does he contradict himself? Why is he so damnably undefinable? My hunch is that he does whatever is appropriate to further the insight of the individual present before him, no matter if that somehow makes the person think of him as a fraud or a god. He really does not care what one thinks of him, you see. At least that is my experience. Just when I think I have Swami pegged, he does something outside my comprehension. When doubt overwhelms me, I later discover why I have learned just as much from that process as when wisdom overwhelms me.

No doubt you are wondering what I mean about sleight of hand. Swami is seated in private with four or five of us, and opens his empty right hand, palm up. He says, 'see it is coming' and in a few seconds, just above his palm, a golden ring appears in mid-air, then falls into his hand. He passes it around. The metal is warm to the touch. Swami tells a story about how changing the heart of man into gold is not his job, but ours, and it takes effort, heat. At that moment a student enters to deliver a message. Swami then very clumsily palms the very ring he had just materialized and we all see him palming it, but he then waves his hand as if creating an object, and (it's no surprise) 'produces' the gold ring, which he gives the student. I could almost feel the student's thoughts 'but... but... but you palmed that!' We all knew the student had not seen it appear in mid-air, and I for one thought surely the boy was now filled with doubts about Swami. 'Why he just palms things!'

Why does he do such things? FIND OUT! Sorry to be so Zen, but that is my experience: one must find out for oneself. After you have seen him and come to know him directly, perhaps your questions about contradictions will be satisfied.

Bon Govanni had put his finger on something that I was beginning to understand. The experience of Sai Baba is unique to every individual. Many people may witness a miracle, but it will mean something completely different to everyone who witnesses it. Sai Baba tells us : 'Seek your own reality. That is what a wise person should do.'

The reality of Sai Baba's miracles was hammered home to me soon after I received the e-mail from Bon Giovanni, during a series of psychic consultations I was doing. A somewhat burly gentleman sat down for his reading and, to my surprise, I noticed that he was wearing a platinum bracelet with a Hindu Om symbol (a sacred symbol that represents the three gods Brahma, Vishnu and Shiva) on it. It seemed completely out of place on such a big man, who I found out later was a builder. I asked him if the bracelet was from Sai Baba and he told me his wonderful story:

I burst into tears when Sai Baba materialized the bracelet for me. He was as close to me as you are now. There was no way it could have been fraud. Swami pointed upward with his finger and I could see a circle of sparkling light swirling above it. Then, to my utter astonishment, I saw the circle of light form into this bracelet hovering in the air six inches above his index finger. Sai Baba then opened his hand and the bracelet dropped into it.

Again, I couldn't help but notice that this big man had tears in the corner of his eyes as he spoke.

Inner transformation

My favourite story was sent to me by Bhupendra Desai, a retired school master who now runs a newsagent's shop in Birmingham and spends all of his spare time painting pictures of Sai Baba. His voice quivers with joy as he tells his story:

> In my opinion Sai Baba's greatest miracle is his ability to cause transformation in our hearts and to awaken our natural divinity. I went to India in 1996 to see Sai Baba with a group of followers. On 20 January I saw him materialize a gold and diamond watch for a young devotee. He then took another devotee's steel ring from his finger and blew on it. We saw it change into a diamond ring. Baba recently also materialized a small Bible containing facts about Jesus. Tears of joy flooded my eyes to see such wonders.
>
> Later I witnessed another marvel. I saw a statue of Sai Baba – as his first incarnation as Shirdi Baba – drink milk from a little pot which was offered by the Hindu priest. In India this is called the *abhishekam* ceremony and your readers may remember how this hit the headlines some time ago when statues, even brass statues, from all over the world started drinking milk. These miracles are interpreted as proof that the formless God can also take form.
>
> The statue of Baba that I saw drinking milk was five feet high and made of solid marble. There was no hollow for the mouth. As it drank the milk I could hear it slurp. It drank half a pot every day.
>
> Recently I was talking to John, a customer at my newspaper shop, about the miracles of Sai Baba and I felt so sorry for him that I gave the man some *vibhuti* ash. Some time ago he had damaged his neck and the doctors said that there was nothing more they could do for him. He had over the years visited many specialists and private doctors.
>
> I gave him four packets of *vibhuti* and a photograph of Sai Baba. The *vibhuti* I gave him had been given to me by Dr D Gadhia, a very old devotee who has been helping teach Baba's teachings about love, truth, right conduct, non-violence and peace. This *vibhuti* was, in fact, extracted from his own body, coming out of his hands and from his legs, particularly at night. This phenomenon lasted for three months and every day devotees from all over the UK were going to his home in

Leicester to see him and would see *vibhuti* everywhere – even in his bed sheets.

I told John to keep these packets under his pillow and under his bed sheet. I also told him to pray to his own chosen God incarnation. I believe he prayed to the Lord Jesus Christ.

John also told me how during the healing process the photo of Sai Baba would move from room to room when his back was turned, yet there were no children or pets in the house that could have done this. This is just one example of healing that Baba can do.

Within a week John could turn his neck 45 degrees. In two weeks he was fully cured and could hold his head straight without any pain. He returned to my shop to thank me. 'It has nothing to do with me,' I said. 'It is Baba who has blessed you.'

Bhupendra Desai sent me many more incredible stories which I am afraid will have to wait for another book. I was beginning to become more and more intrigued by the stories I was receiving from devotees, and the dreams kept reoccurring. My aunt Marion, my father, my sister and even our daughter Danielle dreamed of Sai Baba. I couldn't put it off any longer. I had to go to India to see for myself.

Pilgrimage to India

It was more than curiosity that was calling me. The Spiritualist side of me could quite easily accept the phenomenon of materialization which had already been proved many times in the seance rooms. More importantly, Sai Baba had somehow connected with me on a very deep level of my being. I was still aware of the spirit world and of my guiding spirits but now there was another voice within me, a voice that even the angels bowed down too. I was beginning to believe that Sai Baba really was what he claimed: omnipresent.

I considered my reasons and motives for going to India carefully, and there seemed to be three key issues that I felt I should address. Firstly, we would find out once and for all if Sai Baba really is what he says he is. Secondly, a pilgrimage to India would help us to progress spiritually and hopefully turn us into better people with a clearer understanding of the purpose of life. Thirdly, I needed to know what Sai Baba had to say about the work that people like Jane and myself do. Is it right to communicate with the afterlife? How should we best use our psychic powers? Does reincarnation entail the survival of the individuality? As a Spiritualist I have always believed that the whole human personality, including its memories and character, survives bodily death. Perhaps Sai Baba could help to unify the many aspects of my work which you have read about here. I made a few phone calls and booked to join a small group of four female devotees who would be travelling to the *ashram* in early November.

I will never forget the look of horror on Jane's face as we walked through the airport in Bangalore. Even the swarms of mosquitoes that feasted on our pink flesh appeared to have to fight their way through passport control. I found a trolley that wasn't being slept on and we forced our way to the pre-booked taxi. The cab coughed black smoke and leaped into life, and bounced its way down the pot-holed streets like a uncontrolled kango hammer. Brakes, steering, suspension and windscreen wipers are apparently considered optional accessories in the Bangalore taxi services.

We spent the night in a hotel, and after an extensive shopping trip around the shops of Bangalore with my five female companions, we boarded the taxi again and headed off into the wilds of the countryside. I felt a little guilty at having pressurized Jane into making this journey, but she entered into the spirit of things and her daily worries about new carpets, decorating and DIY now seemed far away. More immediate was the need to know whether we would survive the taxi journey as our scrap car belted at full throttle down the rugged roads to the village of Puttaparthi, or if our luggage would stay on the roof rack. As the car swerved to avoid children, squeezed between juggernauts and sped at oncoming traffic, I learned the spiritual lesson of how to pray with all my heart.

'We're all likely to go through a cleansing process on arrival,' said Carole Alderman, our experienced group leader. 'It tends to happen to most people at first. Don't ask me why, but you may experience some negative feelings.'

I certainly didn't anticipate any problems between anyone in our little group. Jane and I were in good spirits. Carole was a bit bossy, but also a good organizer. Priya was a trainee doctor and radiated compassion. Linda was very easy-going and Annie, a textile designer, was helpful and cheery. We all got on very well. My ego was telling me that I was so spiritually advanced that I would not encounter any problems. So what could Carole possibly mean by saying this?

Even though we were all exhausted with jet lag, Carole urged us to quickly clean and tidy our rooms so that we could catch the afternoon *darshan*. This is held in the *mandir*, a magnificent open-sided temple with wonderful pink, blue and yellow carvings intertwined on its pillars, domes and structure. *Darshan* is a Sanskrit word that means 'the sight of a holy being'. According to the Hindus, just to have sight of a personage with the spiritual magnitude of Sai Baba brings tremendous blessing and triggers a spiritual transformation within the beholder. I was soon to find out what this meant.

As I sat in the line waiting to be led into the *mandir* to view Sai Baba, I listened to the crows squawking overhead and thought about the dream that I had had just prior to leaving England, of arriving at the Prasanthi Nilayam *ashram* by coach and of being immediately called in to see Sai Baba for a private consultation. Was this wish fulfilment or was I going to be called here and now?

In addition, Carole was so convinced that we would have an interview that she drummed into me that I must ask for an interview if I get the opportunity. It was particularly important that I remembered this as Sai Baba usually called groups from the men's side. It was likely that Sai Baba would ask 'How many?' and I must always make sure that everyone in our group was present. 'Six, six, six, don't forget we are six, Craig', said Carole. 'On one occasion Swami asked me the number in my group and I forgot one was ill. I told him the incorrect number and he immediately reprimanded me for my inaccuracy.'

The *darshan* lines are called by drawing lots. I was sitting close to the front of one row and my row was called first. I was led by Sai Baba's *sevadals* (volunteers) to the very front of the area where Sai Baba would walk. We sat for about an hour as everyone else was crammed into the huge building. Then a great hush fell over the crowd and even the birds and monkeys stopped chattering as a small orange form appeared at the far side of the *mandir* where the rest of my group and the other women sat. I could see Sai Baba floating like an orange flower on a sea of silence. Things were happening inside my head that I couldn't begin to explain. All my life I had spoken out against gurus, yet here I sat filled with awe at this person. There were even tears in my eyes. So this is what they meant by *darshan*.

Throughout my life I have been able to see the human aura clearly. As I looked at the little figure in the distance I could see great waves of light pouring from him in every colour imaginable. He seemed to be showering us with light and everyone present could feel it. I saw him speak to a few women on the other side, who got up and walked behind the pillars near the entrance to the inner sanctuary. Other people got up when told to, but I couldn't see if Jane or our group had been called.

Eventually he walked to the area where I was sitting on the floor. He was standing right in front of me and materialized *vibhuti* ash from his fingers and into the hands of devotees nearby. I was so close I could see exactly what was happening just in front of me. The ash was appearing a few inches away from his fingers. 'My God, this is really happening!' Then something happened inside me that is impossible to explain. It was as if something cracked. I could even hear it snap like a silent explosion within. I felt overwhelmed.

Sai Baba walked on, stopping now and again to talk to others, then finally completing his circuit and joining the people who had gathered behind the pillar. The instant he was out of sight most of the crowd rose to their feet and thronged towards the exits. As I turned to leave one of the *sevadals* came up to me and touched my scarf that Carole had given to me to mark out our group. All around there were people wearing scarves from every country of the world. Apparently if one member of a group is called in to see Sai Baba, then all the rest can follow.

'UK? UK?' said the *sevadal* urgently. 'Yes, UK,' I replied, puzzled that he should single me out. 'Your group has been called. Quickly, quickly, follow me. Swami will see you, but you must hurry.' I don't think my heart has ever pounded so hard. Now at last I could ask all my questions. And goodness knew what else would happen. Another *sevadal* joined him and I was rushed towards the front. 'No, No. Too late. Sorry, you miss Swami. Very sorry.'

I walked slowly away from the *mandir* and into the strange unfamiliar world of the *ashram*. This was the story of my life. My biggest grudge is that so often I have come inches away from success, then had the prize whisked away from me at the last minute. There are points in my life when I was nearly a famous artist, nearly a rich man, nearly had my own television show with Jane, nearly met Sai Baba in person. In addition I thought about how so many times people had greatly profited by plagiarizing my ideas, or have stolen my opportunities by jumping on contacts that I had worked hard to establish.

On the *ashram*, time appears to stand still yet also seems so limited. It felt like an eternity that I wandered the *ashram* grounds, contemplating the significance of what had happened. Yet in that short period of time, I resolved a major inner barrier to my personal happiness. In my Spiritualist work as a medium I had always talked about service and Sai Baba is quoted as saying that we should 'give up the fruits of our actions'. So what, if I didn't get the rewards that I believed I deserved? These things are in God's hands. The important thing is that I do my spiritual work and all work in the spirit of service and without thought of reward. Any benefits are just the footprints left in the changing sands of time.

Carole was right about the cleansing process she had said we would go through. Once I had resolved my inner test, I started to feel relief and a growing pleasure at the thought that Jane and our companions had had an interview and I felt eager to know what wonderful things had happened.

'How did it go?' I asked once I'd found them. 'Oh fine,' said Priya, as if it was something that happened every day! 'The interview, what happened in the interview?' I continued. They all looked at me puzzled. 'What interview?' they said, almost in unison. It transpired that there were two UK groups at the *ashram* and that we had identical scarves.

Most people who go to see Sai Baba say that it is the inner transformation that is more remarkable than any physical miracles that Sai Baba performs. Sai Baba gives each visitor an 'inner view' and just like the spirit guides that can communicate to us through our mind, so too does the power of Sai Baba extend into this other dimension of existence. These 'inner views' can take place anywhere, without having to keep visiting the *ashram*. I consequently realized also that a personal interview was perhaps unnecessary. What happens in the *ashram* is a uniquely personal experience and completely subjective, yet relevant to the individual. Everybody who goes discovers something completely different.

Carole had other ideas. From the moment we left she was desperate for a personal interview. This was quite understandable because the last time she had come she was instructed by Sai Baba to write a course for the Sathya Sai Education in Human Values Organization (EHV). This is an integral part of the Indian Education system and is being introduced into schools around the world. The programme has a multi-cultural and multi-faith approach. The system teaches that at the core of all religions lie the same fundamental values by which we should govern our lives. These are right conduct, peace, truth, love and non-violence, which are fundamental in the make-up of the human personality.

Before we left, Carole let me have a look at part of the vast amount of work she had done. On an earlier visit to the *ashram* two years before in 1996 Sai Baba had called her to an interview to approve the first stage:

When he had finished looking through the books he said, 'Very happy. Very happy. Good girl.' During the interview he also turned to me and said 'Where did you get that necklace?' 'You gave it to me, Swami,' I replied. 'Yes,' he smiled. 'I gave it to you last time.'

The gold necklace he was teasing me about was one he had materialized in an interview in November 1995. I had shown him the first book I had written, from which the current books have been born. He had asked if I would promote the Programme in the UK and I had thought, '... but it will be difficult. I will need your help, Swami.' Before the thought had even finished, he had waved his hand and produced a necklace of 101 golden beads with little symbols on them. He then put it over my head and told me never to take it off. And I never have. It is a constant reminder of his presence day and night, reminding me, amongst other things, that he is the doer and I am merely the instrument. I have had so much evidence of this over the last two years that I know I have nothing to worry about, or plan. It all happens as he wills.

Many famous people have visited Sai Baba and come away from the experience feeling that they were not in the presence of an ordinary human being. For example Sarah Ferguson, the Duchess of York, visited the *ashram* and met Sai Baba on 30 January 1997. Although sneered at by the press, Sarah Ferguson had, I discovered, a deeply moving spiritual experience. She was granted a private interview and asked Sai Baba to materialize her a cross and chain. Without hesitation Sai Baba waved his hand and materialized exactly what she asked for. Apparently the Duchess of York was deeply shaken and spiritually inspired by the encounter.

A number of devotees have told me that other celebrity visitors include Rolf Harris, Michael Jackson and Hillary Clinton, but I have not been able to substantiate this fully. In addition, it was widely rumoured that Princess Diana had visited Sai Baba while she was at Bangalore. She sent out a report to the press saying that she wouldn't be attending her engagements due to a throat infection. During this time I am told that she sneaked into the *ashram*.

Shortly after our journey to the *ashram*, Sarah Mills, the daughter of actor Sir John Mills, visited the *ashram* for Christmas. She said of her experience:

Although I never got near him all the time I was in Puttaparthi, I received many real Christmas presents from Sai Baba, none of them costing a penny and all of them changing my life.

Sai Baba is not well served by talk – experiencing him is all. And while I may never go to Puttaparthi again, nor ever understand where the love comes from out there, I do know that that love is truly blinding. How blessed those temple birds are, to be forever surrounded by it.

We too never received a personal interview, but I realize that this was not important. It is what happens inside you that counts. Nonetheless we met many people whose lives had been changed, people who had been healed, and others who had been graced with materialized objects and jewellery. Carole, still desperate for her interview, stayed on for a couple of months after we left. She had been urging us to accept all sorts of austerities in order to win Sai Baba's favour. It hadn't worked. 'Perhaps we should all wear stones in our shoes?' I had joked. However, at the very last *darshan* before Carole had to leave for her flight, Sai Baba came and took her letter. He moved on, then stopped and glanced at her.

'Interview, Swami,' stuttered Carole.

'How many?' replied Sai Baba, pretending not to know.

'Two Swami.'

'TWO!' he teased.

'Yes, husband, Swami.'

'Go,' Sai Baba replied gently. Almost before he had moved on, Carole had picked up her cushion and was running up the aisle to the veranda, tears streaming down her face.

In the interview Sai Baba kept 'accidentally' treading on Carole's toes and spent most of the interview giving all his attention to her husband. (Sai Baba showed his approval of the books by stroking them fondly for 10 to 15 minutes; he had looked through them in an earlier interview with Joan Brake who had taken them for Carole.)

Right up to the last minute Sai Baba was playing his game. Of course he knew how desperate Carole was for an interview. He'd known this all along. As Carole went to go he said, 'Yesterday you were thinking Swami doesn't take my letters. He doesn't look at me, or give me an interview. What can I do? But I am with you always, beside you, above you, around you. I bless, I bless!'

Carole had intended to tell Sai Baba that they were introducing the 'Education in Human Values' programme into many UK schools and would therefore not require a school. But as soon as she thought the words and began to speak Sai Baba interrupted her saying, 'Sathya Sai School. Yes, yes, yes. I bless. I bless.' The huge task that Sai Baba nonchalantly requested is gradually taking shape – but that is another story....

Sai Baba and the afterlife

They say that nobody goes away from the presence of Sai Baba disappointed. I certainly felt inspired and uplifted by the experience and many questions had been answered. But as our time to leave approached, I felt a little sad that I hadn't been able to ask Sai Baba directly about the afterlife and the survival of the human personality after death. Just before we left, a man whom I had not seen before made a casual remark. 'The answer to your questions about the afterlife are to be found in the books by Peggy Mason,' said the stranger. 'She has the answer.' I, of course, wondered how he had known my question, but we were separated by the crowd before I could ask him.

When we returned home we were greeted by our usual mountain of letters. Among them was a package from Peggy Mason. I had read one of her books in the past, and had posted a letter to her sometime ago. Nonetheless, it seemed very odd that it should arrive perfectly on cue. She had enclosed all the information she had about Sai Baba and the afterlife, writing:

> Of course reincarnation entails the survival of the individuality. One of my favourite quotes of Baba's: 'The good fortune that has brought you face to face with me is something for which you must thank your merit won through previous lives.'
>
> Baba knew, of course, that for many years my late husband (Ron Lang) and I had the most gifted medium living in our staff cottage when we had a big place near Crowborough. For 14 years I wrote monthly articles for the Spiritualist magazine *Two Worlds* when Maurice Barbanell was editor. As many people are so ignorant about mediumship and the continuation of the individual after leaving the physical body, we made a point of asking Baba, in private interview, for the sake of other people, 'Is mediumship, to communicate with those in the next sphere of life, provided the medium is honest and a pure channel, wrong?
>
> Baba replied at once: 'No, not at all.'

Peggy Mason included a wealth of material, none of which conflicts with what I have tried to communicate through this book. The full details will have to wait for another book. Peggy went on to explain that she was still in touch with her husband via an excellent trance medium, Paul Bura. She concluded by saying:

My husband Ron is of course longing for me to join him! He has it all prepared, and has a lovely little house by a lake, and our beloved sheepdog, Tippy, with him and my cat, Peter (and adds: 'and you don't have to feed them!'). He works with a group of spirits helping those 'without a clue, wondering what on earth has happened to them' as he puts it, go over.

When I asked him what it was like to be received by Baba when he passed over, he said, 'like being embraced by the Universe'. He also says he and Baba will come for me. My health is running down, plus angina, etc. so I don't expect to be here beyond next summer....

A few weeks later I read in *Psychic News* that Peggy Mason had died.

Chapter Eleven

Conclusion and frequently asked questions

According to a MORI survey conducted in 1998 to assess how many people believed in God or the paranormal across the UK, more than nine out of ten people – an astonishing 92 per cent of the population – believe in the paranormal, yet only 64 per cent believe in God. The pollsters also discovered that four out of ten people believe in ghosts, and one in seven claim to have experienced a sighting. Six out of ten people believe in premonitions, 30 per cent are convinced dreams can tell the future, and 54 per cent say telepathy works. Over half of the UK population have experienced *déjà vu*. Also, just over ten percent have been to a fortune-teller, the same number who have been to a medium. Eight per cent say the future has been predicted to them in a dream and eight per cent have visited a faith healer. I understand that the figures for America are even higher than those from the UK.

Today many people are seeking answers to their spiritual questions and turning to people like myself for answers. To conclude, here are a few of the most frequently asked questions that I receive, along with my answers which are based upon my experience of mediumship and clairvoyance. I may yet be wrong in many of my conclusions, but I believe that we are beginning at least to ask the right questions.

Is everybody psychic?

There are many people who are openly antagonistic to people who claim to be psychic. Many of these individuals would deny the evidence, no matter how overwhelmingly in favour, of the existence of ESP. In this vendetta it seems that scientists and fundamentalist Christians share the common goal of discrediting the claims of psychics for, if what we say is true, then their beliefs will be shaken to the very foundations. A person who is really in search of the truth is not upset if it turns out to be different from their preconceptions.

Those who deny their psychic powers suppress them, but that is not to say that these unused gifts are not still latent within them. I believe that everyone has latent psychic powers, and may even have latent powers of materialization. With the growing acceptance of psychic powers, the phenomenon will continue to grow stronger. Many people believe that we are entering a New Age of expanded consciousness and that we will witness incredible things in the coming years.

Can I increase my latent psychic powers?

I have found that I can train most open-minded people to develop ESP, but only a few are able to develop their mediumistic skills. Psychic development works best within a group or a Spiritualist circle. In this environment there is much more energy to work with and the support of everyone around gives people the confidence to advance. The collective power of a group of people working together is greater than the sum total of each person's energy. A list of techniques and organizations can be found in my previous book *The Psychic Workbook* (Vermilion, 1995).

Are psychic powers and spirituality related?

Unfortunately, all types of people can be psychic. Rasputin, for example, had the power to hypnotize people from a distance, yet he was a man of evil intent. The Fox sisters were Spiritualism's most important mediums, yet they were uneducated country girls. Helen Duncan was an incredible materialization medium, yet her manner was coarse and sometimes vulgar. Psychic powers may spontaneously occur in people who have attained a high degree of spiritual development, but powers are not necessarily proof of good character. Just because someone has a beautiful voice that can move people to tears, it does not mean that they are a beautiful person.

Can we change the future?

Our destiny is decided by our karma. Fortunately we can get rid of bad karma by good inner and outer behaviour. The best way to change the future for the better is to change ourselves. The power of free will can be directed outwardly into the world to bring us worldly things, but becomes most effective when we direct it at ourselves to bring about an inner transformation. This is the highest way to change our destiny. Therefore, the objective of fortune-telling should be to give the sitter the guidance so that they can find spiritual solutions to their material worries. In this way even a negative destiny can be reversed. In short, it is not about telling the future; it is about changing the future.

What happens after death?

At brain death we shed the physical body as we would a suit of clothes, and progress to the spirit world in our astral body. This is a temporary form and is made of a material that is on a higher vibration to gross matter. As we progress we shed this etheric sheath and enter into the realms of pure spirit which is indescribable in earthly terms; the closest metaphor for this state is that it is a 'world of light'.

At the point of death some people are aware of the material world but most fall into the 'tunnel of light' that is often described by people who have come back from the brink of death. People who have undergone a near-death experience usually describe reaching a demarcation point (sometimes symbolized by a fence, pearly gates or a stairway). Once this threshold has been crossed there is no returning to the physical body. We are greeted by those we love who have gone before us and we become aware of God who appears to us in the form we are most familiar with. An atheist or Buddhist may experience God as a light, a Hindu may see Krishna, a Moslem may see Mohammed or the light of Allah and a Christian may see the form of Jesus.

Does the human personality survive death?

Mediumship indicates that the personality, with all its quirks, idiosyncrasies and memories, survives death. It is reassuring to know that the dead we love continue in the next world. They remain just as we knew them but minus their physical ailments.

This is not the final spiritual goal – for what is the personality? Who are you? The personality is only the outer trappings of something greater, it is not your quintessence. The goal of human life is to realize our divinity, to merge directly with the God within us. A Buddhist will tell you that the personality and the self are illusions. The real you is the consciousness within, which is never born into either the material world or the heavenly world. The best place to realize this inner divinity is here on earth and the spirit planes should be considered as just a sojourn between lives.

Will I meet the people I dislike, such as my ex-marital partner, in the next world?

Like attracts like. In the spirit world you will come together with those you love most and who you are bound to by a higher 'over-self'. The people who have troubled you in life will go their own way. However, when the purpose of your life is revealed to you, then you may see that the negative people were sent to test you for a specific reason. Despite the pain they have caused, you may understand that they are not evil, but were sent so that you may flower spiritually. God gives his hardest tests to his most advanced pupils.

How do you square the idea of reincarnation with the Spiritualist evidence for an afterlife?

You have read a number of stories in this book that suggest that reincarnation is a fact, and yet have also read of cases that suggest that there is an afterlife. Although these two ideas may seen diametrically opposed, I believe that both beliefs can be brought together as one. The Hindus believe that everyone has an eternal soul called the *Jiva*. It has never been born and can exist forever – a concept similar to the Spiritualist fourth principle of 'the continuous existence of the human soul'. The *Jiva's* nature is innately pure, but by evil deeds it has become clothed in ignorance. After death the *Jiva* leaves the material body and goes to the solar regions of which there are spheres upon spheres. (This corresponds with the 'many mansions' of Christianity, the spheres of the afterlife as described by Spiritualists, or the *Bardos* of the Tibetan Buddhists).

The earth is the world sphere in which there are moons, suns and stars, but beyond this is the lunar sphere and beyond that is the sphere of lightning. In this high realm the *Jiva* is taken to the highest heaven called the *Brahmaloka* where it can live for eternity and never be born or die again. Only the perfected souls who have given up all desires can live in this exalted state. This differs somewhat from the Spiritualist precept that there is 'eternal progress open to every human soul', which suggests that there is no final goal to existence.

The lower souls may enter the lunar sphere as an angelic being where they may enjoy a prolonged period of happiness, but this lasts only for as long as the effect of their good deeds endures. Once this good karma is exhausted it descends again into the earth sphere and takes a new human birth. The person in the spirit world dies and is reborn in human form. Also, in these realms there is a hierarchy of beings which corresponds with the spiritualist principle of the 'Ministry of Angels'. Furthermore, the idea that our sojourn in the spirit world is dictated by our karma corresponds with the Spiritualist belief that we must take 'personal responsibility' for our destiny.

In short, I believe that our stay in the afterlife is only temporary. While in these ethereal worlds, we accumulate neither good nor bad karma. However, our period in the afterlife is fuelled by the karma accumulated on earth prior to our death. When the soul's good karma is worked out, then the remaining karma begins to take effect, and the soul comes down to earth to become a human again. If the person continues to do spiritual work and purifies himself, then they may finally go to *Brahmaloka* and need come back no more.

Do animals have psychic powers?

There is evidence to suggest that animals display a range of psychic powers. Animals with psychic powers have a greater chance of survival than those without them. Telepathy can be useful to give warnings to the herd about predators, while clairvoyance helps animals find their way or locate the whereabouts of water. Precognition helps animals anticipate an attack, and a sensitivity to vibration helps them to 'smell death' in places that are dangerous or to know when a place is safe. And some animals stroke their fellow creatures when they are ill – indicating perhaps a desire to heal.

However, there is a higher function of psychic powers which is unique to humans. Just as Sai Baba has the power to materialize objects, appear in two places at once and perform the impossible, so too these powers are within reach of every human being. Once we awaken the higher spiritual forces, reality itself changes and we can perform acts that the materialist would consider impossible. It is only in the human form that we can attain this state of being.

Do animals survive death?

I believe that there are two sorts of animals: those that have an individual consciousness and those that are part of a group consciousness. Pets develop a greater sense of identity because of their contact with humans. Although their behaviour is mostly instinctive, they also appear to gain a certain degree of self-awareness. They may have also experienced love. I believe that these influences help form an individual soul that retains its sense of identity after death. I am reminded of one lady who came for a mediumistic consultation: 'Don't tell me anything about the humans over there,' she said. 'I only want to know about my cats.' I was able to give her the names of all eight of her cats and character traits that each had. Although I believe I had her 'dead' father helping me, it proved to me that some animals survive death and, like us, retain their character-istics beyond the grave.

I also believe, although I have no empirical proof of this belief, that most animals merge into the collective consciousness of their species after their death.

Can animals take human birth?

Metempsychosis is a theory dating from before the ancient Greeks that says that every living thing reincarnates. In the course of time the animal becomes man. It is interesting to note that the human popula-tion is increasing while the animal population is decreasing. Perhaps these animal souls are all becoming human? The Tibetan Buddhists emphasize how important and rare it is to have a 'precious human birth' – because we live for such a long time in animal form, a human birth, bringing with it a chance to attain enlightenment, is a tremen-dous opportunity. I personally find it fascinating to watch people's behaviour and observe their animal characteristics. Some people pout like fish, while others slink like cats or charge ahead like bulls. How many people do you know that chatter like birds, eat like pigs or behave like rats?

Can aliens take human birth?

I have met 'mediums' who have spoken with a high-pitched, squeaky voice, and claim that an alien is speaking through them. So far I am completely unconvinced by what I have seen and heard, although I believe that it is inevitable, given the size of the universe, that there is life on other planets. I cannot answer this question with any authority. However, Sai Baba was asked this same question and said that alien life reincarnates in its own star system and that they have their own afterlife worlds.

Will I always find the people I love?

People who love each other share their karma. I believe that there exists a group soul of which our individual selves are emanations. Soul mates can include parents, family, children and friends, as well as lovers and partners. Those that love each other will be drawn together in the afterlife and in future earthly lives.

Who are the spirit guides?

It is possible that the spirit guides may be aspects of our own psychology that have become disassociated from the personality and taken on a life of their own. They could also be what the Tibetans call *tulpas*, which are genie-like beings created by the concentrated power of thought. However, I believe that the spirit guides are real beings that come to help us. I have come to this conclusion because my own spirit guides have supplied me with evidence of their reality via the mouthpiece of other mediums. All of us have a spirit guide which some call the guardian angel.

Is there a Hell?

When Christianity spread throughout Europe it supplanted the ancient pagan gods and built its churches upon their most sacred sites. Everything associated with these old religions was branded as evil. For example, Pan was traditionally a cloven-footed god of fertility who brought happiness and jollity. The Christians supplanted him with the evil figure of the devil and lord of Hell.

There is no inescapable Hell as such, but Spiritualists believe that the afterlife consists of many spheres of existence, some of which are 'lower' planes. All souls are innately divine but can become corrupted by their evil deeds. The heaviness of their vibration makes them sink like a stone to the lower spheres. Here they are guided by wise souls to reform their ways and, in time, given another chance at life – possibly in animal form.

It is interesting to note how close Spiritualist ideas are to the Hindu beliefs. In the *Vedas* (the ancient sacred writings of Hinduism) there is no mention of Hell but in the *Puranas* (the later books) these regions are described in detail. Here the bad karma is worked out through pain and suffering, but mercifully the offender is finally given another chance at life on earth.

What is the reason for suffering?

Joy leads to complacency and often sorrow is our greatest teacher. Both come to us because of the karma generated by our actions. However, the middle way leads to realization of our divinity and the release from suffering.

What is the purpose of life?

To realize that we are One.

Acknowledgements

Thank you to all the people who have been prepared to come forward and tell their stories in the knowledge that their very personal experiences may help others realize that psychic phenomena are real and that there is life after death. In many cases I have changed the names of people to protect their privacy.

Do you have a psychic story?

The author can be contacted on the internet: http://psychics.co.uk or by letter via the publisher.

Index

hunting tribes 38
Huxley, Aldous 135
Hyde, Elizabeth 128–30
hypnagogic dreaming 66–7

India 167–73

Jackson, Michael 11, 114, 172
Jagger, Mick 115
Jameson, Ellen 36, 37
Jenkins, Stephen 60
Jiva 179–80
Johnson, Winnie 32–3
Joshi, Baskher and Hema 161–3
Jung, Carl 74–5

karma 84, 142–3, 178, 180, 183
King, Richard 143–4
King, William Lyon Mackenzie 121
Kitt, Eartha 118
Knowles, Nick 33–4
Koestler, Arthur 43, 73
Kopec, Stan, Karen and Kalle 10–14
Kübler-Ross, Elizabeth 128

Lang, Cosmo Gordon 19
Late Night Live 29
Lennon, John 118
ley lines 60, 102–3
Liberace, Lee 114, 116
light 104, 130, 178
Lodge, Joan 48
Looe Bar, Cornwall 60
Lorelei 143–4

lottery winnings 65, 87
love 38–42, 182
Lucas, Jackie 93–4
lucid dreams 62, 154

McCallum, Amanda 149–50
MacLaine, Shirley 117
MacMillan, Harry 59–60
Madeley, Richard 29
The Magic and Mystery Show 33–4, 137
Martin, David 53–4
Martin, Mary 152–3
Martin, Stuart 16
Mason, Peggy 174–5
materialization 158, 160, 162, 164–6, 172
 see also vibhuti
Mathews, Jenny and Brett 123
mediumship 10–37, 18–21
Medway Dr 107–8
Messing, Wolf 121
metempsychosis 181
Mignonette 68, 71, 72
Mills, Sarah 172–3
Mills, Sir John 172
miracles 154–75
Mitchell, Edgar 41
Moody, Anny 102
Moody, Raymond 128
Moon, Keith 114
MORI belief survey 176
Morris, Bob 86–7

The Narrative of Arthur Gordon Pym of Nantucket 70–1

soul, progress concept 133–5, 180

soul mates 143–4, 182

spirit guides 135–40, 182

spirits and angels 76–113

spiritual healing 116–17

Spiritualist church 18–19, 105

Spottiswood, Di 100–1

Stafford, Bridgitte 48–9

Stalin, Joseph 121

Stephens, Edwin 68–70, 72

Sting 115–16

Stokes, Doris 9, 15–18, 36, 37

Stokes, John 16–18

Stokes, Rosemary and Ray 88

Stokes, Terry 16, 17

Stone, Jannet 148–9

Stuart, Debbie 94–6

suffering 183

Sutcliffe, Peter 55

Swanson, Gloria 117

Swayze, Patrick 117

synchronicity 73–4

T., Jennifer 61–2

Taratha (spirit helper) 137

Tarot Cards 27, 36

Taylor, Elizabeth 116

Taylor, Kevin 149–50

telepathy 38–51, 176

television 28–37

Tennant, Neil 114–15

This Morning (TV programme) 29

time 53–67, 74, 117–18, 176, 178

Turoff, Stephen 162

UFOs 118, 164

vibhuti 154, 161–3, 166–7, 170

Vorderman, Carol 34

Walton, David 16–17

war 50, 63–4, 102, 119–22, 145, 146

West, Fred and Rosemary 32

Williams, Keith 19

Wiseman, Dr Richard 33–4

Woodhouse, Barbara 50

Yates, Paula 28

York, Michael 117